RUSSIAN FOOD SINCE 1800

Marina Mogilner, Associate Professor, University of Illinois at Chicago, USA
Willard Sunderland, Henry R. Winkler Professor of Modern History, University of Cincinnati, USA

Published Titles

Upcoming Titles

RUSSIAN FOOD SINCE 1800

EMPIRE AT TABLE

Catriona Kelly

BLOOMSBURY ACADEMIC
LONDON • NEW YORK • OXFORD • NEW DELHI • SYDNEY

BLOOMSBURY ACADEMIC
Bloomsbury Publishing Plc
50 Bedford Square, London, WC1B 3DP, UK
1385 Broadway, New York, NY 10018, USA
29 Earlsfort Terrace, Dublin 2, Ireland

BLOOMSBURY, BLOOMSBURY ACADEMIC and the Diana logo are
trademarks of Bloomsbury Publishing Plc

First published in Great Britain 2024

Series design by Tjaša Krivec
Cover image: Nikolai Kichunov, *Market Gardening and
Commercial Berry-Growing Outside Petrograd*, 1914

A catalogue record for this book is available from the British Library.

A catalog record for this book is available from the Library of Congress.

ISBN:	HB:	978-1-3501-9277-5
	PB:	978-1-3501-9278-2
	ePDF:	978-1-3501-9279-9
	eBook:	978-1-3501-9280-5

Typeset by Integra Software Services Pvt. Ltd.
Printed and bound in Great Britain

To find out more about our authors and books visit www.bloomsbury.com
and sign up for our newsletters.

I teach the art of eating, not drinking, for tutors of the latter are easy to find

–Vladimir Odoevsky, 1845.

In our motherland no-one goes hungry

–*The Book of Tasty and Nutritious Food, 1939.*

CONTENTS

ILLUSTRATIONS

ABBREVIATIONS AND CONVENTIONS

RGIA: Russian State Historical Archive, St Petersburg.

RKTB: *Russkie krest'yane: zhizn', byt, nravy: Materialy 'Etnograficheskogo byuro' knyazya V. N. Tenisheva,* ed. D. A. Baranov and A. V. Konovalov (St Petersburg: Rossiiskii etnograficheskii muzei, 2004, and continuing).

SBU HA: Central Archive of the Ukrainian Security Service, Kyiv.

TsGA-SPb.: Central State Archive, St Petersburg.

TsGAIPD-SPb: Central State Archive of Documents in Political History, St Petersburg.

Where otherwise not indicated, material from diaries and memoirs comes from the online searchable database Prozhito.ru.

Soft and hard signs (' and ") are omitted from Russian transliterations in the main text, but included in notes and bibliographical references.

Complete source notes, a list of historical cookbooks, and an expanded list of further reading, as well as a selection of Russian recipes and food photographs, are available on https://www.bloomsburyonlineresources.com/russian-food-since-1800.

ACKNOWLEDGEMENTS

On my first visit to Russia in 1979, I lived in a student hostel and ate canteen food. I remember the shock of turning the tap of an urn marked 'Coffee' and unleashing pale-brown liquid (milk and sugar weren't optional). Our base was the prestigious Polytechnic in Leningrad, so the food was adequate, though so low in vitamins that after two and a half weeks I developed a quinsy and needed urgent medical treatment. Since then, I have usually bought and prepared food myself – for nearly twenty years now, in my own kitchen in St Petersburg. I have developed a love of black bread, smoked fish, wood mushrooms, unrefined sunflower oil, sour cream, fresh and pickled vegetables, berries and fruit imported from the south, and of Georgian, Ukrainian, Belorussian, Central Asian and Baltic food as well as Russian. Indeed, if you want 'traditional Russian', a Belorussian restaurant is probably your best bet.

Generous friends have also fed me, sharing meals at the kitchen table, or, for larger parties, at a table in a room that usually has another function. Even these days, most Russians don't have the space for chilly, wan rooms used only for formal meals. Food should be abundant, enjoyable and accompanied by talk. From these meals and people's stories about their experience, I have learned at least as much as from written sources. I am grateful to them all, to those who have attended my talks (and often argued with what I've said), to my many Facebook friends and real-life friends for suggestions, particularly Marina Samsonova and Sasha Grigorieva, and to the authors of the sources, both primary and secondary, that I cite (a selection of the latter appears in the List of Further Reading at the end).

INTRODUCTION: CABBAGE SOUP AND OYSTERS

Food matters in Russia. Eating and politics are closely intertwined. To feed is also to rule.[1] People's sense of home is inseparable from what they eat. Soviet spy Konon Molodyi, preparing to pose as Canadian businessman Gordon Lonsdale, parted bitterly from the delights of the Russian diet. 'I had to force myself to forget everything I had once loved: dark ryebread, milk fresh out of the cow, cabbage soup, borshch with thick sour cream, forest mushrooms and berries, the fragrant cabbage pies that we baked at home for all occasions and none … '

Homesickness and regret for the lost past alike focus on food. Outsiders fixate on the long lines for basic products that were common in the Soviet period. Insiders see food in terms of joy, celebration and communitarian sharing. Yet Russia has a long history of self-denial too, shown in radicals' indifference to gastronomy as well as the Russian Orthodox Church's exigent fasts. Food-inspired disgust can be as powerful as Proustian reverie. Take poet Timur Kibirov's olfactory world in a 1987 poem with the sarcastic title, 'Through Tears of Parting': canteen whiffs swirl alongside frowsy hostel beds, haphazardly bleached lavatories, and clouds of harsh tobacco. Food is the focus of ambivalent emotions, including rage and distress as well as pleasure and enjoyment; comfort and love mingle with envy and frustration.

There are still people in today's Russia for whom starvation is a living memory. Museum displays commemorating the Siege of Leningrad highlight the tiny ration of bread, adulterated with sawdust and weeds, that was the sole diet for many city-dwellers during the terrible winter of 1941–2, when over half a million died. In 1891, crop failures caused by severe weather killed comparable numbers; a still more serious famine (around 5 million dead) occurred in 1921–2, exacerbated by the social collapse of revolution and war. Over the years 1931–2, between 7 and 12 million perished as a result of grain and livestock requisitions during the forced collectivization of the countryside. Russia's most recent famine came as late as 1946–7.

Yet even at the most terrible times, food consumption was not simply about staying alive. During the Siege, Leningrad factories produced foodstuffs not essential to survival, such as sweets and chocolates. Diaries recorded dreams of luxuriant meals. Food is the most basic human need, but eating amounts to much more than nutrition. Privilege, but also self-expression and sheer delight, are all possible associations.

The foods that can evoke emotional responses aren't always those with long roots. The history of Russian food is also the history of receptiveness to new eating experiences. As in other countries, imports from abroad and the mechanization of food production wrought fundamental changes to eating practices. In one sense 'Russian food' applies to a diet mainly comprising grain, sour milk products, river fish, potatoes and cabbage – as still served in the refectories of Russian monasteries. In another it means the entire panoply of what Russians actually ate in the past, and what they eat now – and the accompanying shifts in social practices.

Food is not an abstraction; it is part of the material world. A discussion that focused simply on its ideological function would be as dry and unsatisfying to the reader as the rusks (sukhariki) that Russians traditionally stockpiled to be eaten when all else failed. To understand food history, you need to grasp the symbolic meaning of food, the social practices that created it, the actual foods consumed and their emotional resonance – as sketched in the 'food panorama' that follows.

Patriotic eating

Because food and national identity are so tightly associated, 'Russian food' is a meaningful expression in the way that 'British food' (in contrast to English, Scottish, Welsh and Northern Irish) isn't. A standard argument holds that Russia's long history as an empire effaced the country's character as a nation state. When it comes to diet, things are different. In *Anna Karenina*, Konstantin Levin, the Tolstoyan landowner who insists on living in the country and helping with the mowing, demonstratively opts for cabbage soup at dinner in an expensive restaurant. His future brother-in-law, Stiva Oblonsky, luxuriates in a plate of oysters. Levin will be faithful to Kitty; Stiva has deceived Dolly with the French governess. Choice of diet is part of a moral pattern.

These presumptions and prejudices were a century old when Tolstoy was writing. Already in the eighteenth century, Russian patriots railed (like their English counterparts) against 'fancy foreign messes'. 'The tables were not as they were in the olden days, when people used only the produce of their own households. They endeavoured to infuse their meat and fish with alien seasonings', raged Prince Mikhail Shcherbatov in his 1787 tract, *On the Ruination of Morals in Russia*. 'Our dining rooms do not greet the guest with fumes and the aroma of food, but the pure, fresh air provokes an appetite in him who enters; his eye is not met by pralines, pâtés, and pyramids as objects requiring admiration, but every dish is prepared with elegance and taste, and in such a way that each can easily help himself as he desires' was the boast of I. M. Radetsky in *The Gourmet's Almanac* sixty-five years later.

The emergence of modern Russian national consciousness was rooted in food. Sincere feeling for the homeland meant rejection of alien diet. There was a direct line between Russian eighteenth-century merchants objecting to the importation of delicacies, and the counter-sanctions against the European Union in post-2014 Russia, as mountains of suspect cheese were ploughed by bulldozers into the mud.

The idea that home-produced food – simple and natural – was under threat from the aggressive imperialism of external powers, particularly in Western Europe and America, resurfaced with a vengeance in the post-Soviet period, as decades of near-isolation from non-native produce came to an end. 'NO TO *COLA*NISATION: KVAS IS THE HEALTH OF THE NATION' punned an early twenty-first-century poster for a traditional Russian soft drink. But gastro-patriotism did not inhibit a 'foodie boom'. The culinary sections of bookstores occupied more space even than management guides, grooming manuals and translated romances. There was fancy cooking of the TV chef variety (UK stars Gordon Ramsey and Jamie Oliver dominated these shelves, among foreigners). But there were also user-friendly family albums and po-faced, nerdy guides bristling with special equipment and microscopically detailed guidance.

Cultural centralization during the Stalin era imposed a constrictive repertoire on most areas of creativity. Cooking was no exception. Just as everyone read Pushkin in school and listened to Tchaikovsky on the radio, so the New Year table was graced with Salad Olivier, a chopped potato salad with a (usually bottled) mayonnaise dressing. But diversity extends backwards as well as forwards. It's a shock to realize, from pre-1917 cookbooks, menus, diaries, literary sources and post-factum testimony, just how varied Russian cooking once was. Milk products from Vologda, chickens from Yaroslavl, fruit and wine from the south were all common in markets and on tables. Gavrila Derzhavin's tribute to Catherine II, *Felitsa* (1783) complimented the Empress for her own modest diet, but showed one of her courtiers feasting on sturgeon and caviar from Astrakhan as well as Westphalian ham and 'Strasbourg pie' with foie gras.[2] Edith Sollohub, born in 1886, remembered in *The Russian Countess* not just elegant boxes of expensive sweets from Conradi's in St Petersburg, or the rich kulich loaves and sweet curd cheese paskha of the Easter table, but 'my old Niania who was from the far north and could make delicious pancakes and buns out of the simplest rye flour with sour cream and a little butter.'[3]

During the Soviet period, choice – where people could exercise it – tended to be driven more by the reputation of particular factories (Red October and Krupskaya chocolate, say) than regional factors. After 1991, Russia rediscovered its geographical diversity. When I was a student during the Brezhnev era in Voronezh, about 600 km south-east of Moscow, you couldn't buy meat in the ordinary state shops. You had to join a long line for roughly hacked, oozing slabs of carcass in the collective farm market, not far from the city's main square. This market, with fruit, fresh and dried, from the Caucasus and Central Asia, and Cuban oranges as well as curd cheese and sour cream from local farms, was as colourful as the main shops were grey. But it was much too expensive for everyday shopping (one lemon cost the equivalent of 10 dollars, calculated by proportion of average income). In the twenty-first century, Voronezh became a major centre of quality meat and milk production. Its enormous brand-new market won a national prize as best shopping mall of 2018. Premium products still went for premium prices, but the range had expanded beyond all recognition.

Modern food cultures are dynamic. American eating was transformed by products such as corn flakes and Jell-O, whether as an aspic substitute or salad ingredient.[4] Pasta, pizza and olive oil became 'Italian national foods' during the late nineteenth century.[5] In twentieth-century Russia, mayonnaise – used to top fish and meat as well as to dress salads – became comparably ubiquitous. On 31 March 1981, writer Igor Dedkov saw groups of women in Kostroma continue queuing for mayonnaise even after ice fell off a roof and killed or maimed several of those in line. On 20 December 1988, journalist Yuri Pominov named mayonnaise, alongside buckwheat and macaroni, as one of three essentials to life that were chronically scarce. Yet mayonnaise (then known as sauce provençale) had no national associations before 1917. Its rise to favour was a triumph of the Second Five-Year Plan (1933–8). Collectivization, however brutally, had ensured a supply of basic foods to the cities. Now the population could be fed more generously. City-dwellers, or a proportion of them, were regularly reminded of the new opportunities by posters, leaflets and cookbooks. Most famous among the last was *The Book of Tasty and Nutritious Food*, first issued in 1939, reprinted in abridged and simplified editions during the 1940s, then relaunched in full-colour form in 1952, after which came almost annual reprints, half a million at a time – but still never enough to sate demand.

The state will provide

State control over food production is universal in modern societies. The USSR was unusual in that intervention extended not just to quality regulation, and to the promotion of healthy ways of cooking and eating, but to ownership of agricultural land (nationalized the day after the Bolsheviks took power), and food production and distribution. There was a history of state involvement before 1917. Large numbers of peasants were themselves 'owned' by the state (42 per cent in 1858). Government investment was central to the development of agriculture in the Russian steppes. State-sponsored projects, such as land grants and the development of the railways, had a direct impact on food distribution.[6] Research in agriculture, particularly grain-growing, was steered by the internationally recognized Bureau of Applied Botany under the Ministries of Agriculture and of State Property, which had built up an impressive seed bank by the 1910s. Thanks in part to these initiatives, output of food, both for export and the domestic population, improved significantly between the late 1880s and the start of the First World War, as even Soviet commentators acknowledged in the 1920s.

Once the First World War began, the Imperial Russian state also made interventions into food distribution, through requisition at one end and rationing systems at the other. But in peacetime, food was sold in small shops, at market stalls or by hawkers in streets and courtyards (see Figure 0.1 below). Villagers likewise used fairs and markets, and also non-monetary systems of exchange (milk bartered for vegetables, say, or bread and soup for help with the harvest).

Private trading in food never disappeared completely under Soviet power. The New Economic Policy (NEP, 1921–8) permitted activity by private entrepreneurs in the food marketing and service sectors. At times, administrators facilitated private trade. In 1923, the city authorities opened an official market on Kuznechnyi pereulok, Petrograd, where an improvised one had sprung up during the late 1910s.

Markets continued to exist legally throughout the Soviet period, and it was here that collective and state farmers sold the produce of their carefully tended private plots. Wild birds and animals shot by hunters were also marketed outside the state system, on a cooperative basis.[7] There was also a grey economy: shop workers selling food from under the counter (at a markup to themselves), or state farm workers touting produce round high-rise estates. Even in big cities, scarcities circulated by barter: a jar of Bulgarian peas, say, swapped for a packet of Hungarian bacon.

Figure 0.1 Child hawkers in Moscow, 1859. Charles Piazzi Smyth. (Courtesy Royal Observatory of Edinburgh.)

But if the state's control was never total, it expanded enormously compared with the situation pre-1917. The All-Soviet Academy of Agriculture, founded in 1929, presided over a vast network of nationwide research institutions. A constellation of institutes specializing in applied food science aimed to balance the objectives of nutrition, economy and popularity. State vending outlets were everywhere, from kiosks and vending machines up to elephantine 'gastronom' stores. And most people living in the USSR believed in the state's obligation to provide them with food, an obligation that extended to distribution through the workplace.

A key slogan was 'To each according to his need'. But it was not so much need in the sense of nutritional or medical requirements, as political and social standing that counted. According to the principles of rationing established in 1918, manual workers had bigger rations than non-manual workers. While this had a calorific justification, administrative workers were also privileged, being assigned to Category 2. The intelligentsia and free professions comprised Category 3, and the 'bourgeoisie' (traders, rentiers etc.) made up Category 4. Similar categories operated during the war.

'People of the middle state'

At all eras, what you ate was directly dependent on social status. The better-off (in villages as well as small towns and cities, and among manual workers as well as non-manual) ate more of everything, and significantly more meat, fish, milk products, vegetables and fruit. This was consistent both before and after 1917.[8]

Nineteenth-century Russian cookbooks regularly included sections of 'food for servants', in which animal products figured sparingly, and priority was given to simplicity and bulk. Ekaterina Avdeeva's *The Handbook of the Experienced Russian Housewife*, first published in 1842, recommended soups (tripe, potato, cabbage), sheep's head, kasha, noodles and fruit kissel. *Encyclopaedia of the Experienced Russian Housewife* by 'Boris Volzhin' (Vladimir Burnashov), also published in 1842, added liver and tripe stew and offal soup. (Their British contemporary, Eliza Acton, provided no comparable advice in *Modern Cookery for Private Families*, 1845.)

In the real world, officers and 'other ranks' in the armed forces were fed separate diets; the only members of privileged social strata whose diet approximated that of servants were pupils in closed institutions such as boarding schools, orphanages and military colleges. Adult visitors were taken aback. 'There were pies stuffed with rice for breakfast!!' exclaimed Vladimir Telyakovsky, visiting the Imperial Theatre College in March 1900. 'I don't think that's very suitable.'

The sector of society that took the most intense interest in food was evoked by Avdeeva: 'I shall address myself not to the higher ranks, but to the daily life of people of the middle state.' Indeed, the 'middle state', an amalgam of social layers that embraced the more impecunious nobility and gentry as well as merchants, the better-off educated townspeople, and (by the late nineteenth century) successful peasant entrepreneurs, became the producers and consumers of a Russian 'cuisine bourgeoise': restrained rather than extravagant, open to innovation yet at the same time respectful of convention, concerned with integrity rather than show, and sensitive to regional nuance.[9]

Among the champions of this style of cooking was Prince Vladimir Odoevsky, the author of *Lectures of Doctor Puf*, published in a supplement to *Literary Gazette* from 1844 to 1845. His menus promoted simplicity. Even 'a chic dinner worthy of the gentry' for Doctor Puf's birthday comprised just six courses: pea soup with rice, vols-aux-vents, roast veal, fish in aspic, roast blackcock and bought-in pudding. Simpler still was the excellent meal that Puf ate as the guest of a cultivated family of merchants: cabbage soup, roast beef with roast potatoes and green beans, woodcock on toast and home-made fruit paste (marmelad). The wines were St Julien and Graves, 'which is much better than chilly Château Lafite or warm champagne'.

As Russia boomed in the late nineteenth and early twentieth centuries, the 'middle state' developed more elaborate tastes. The most widely reprinted cookbooks of the era, Elena Molokhovets's *A Gift for Young Housewives* (twenty-nine editions between 1861 and 1917) and Praskovya Aleksandrova-Ignatyeva's *The Practical Foundations of the Culinary Art* (twelve editions between 1899 and 1927) were more ambitious as well as more voluminous than their predecessors. They ran to hundreds of recipes, many with lavish ingredients. During the Leningrad Siege, readers pored with cynicism or wonderment over Molokhovets's references to, say, pears Duchesse. Yet, by the 1880s, Molokhovets's visions paled by comparison with habits among the well-off. Tchaikovsky noted in 1887 how a friend, suffering from a temporary ailment, downed two bowls of soup, an entire black sole and two baked apples – and told his doctor with a clear conscience that he'd eaten 'nothing at all'. The British writer Stephen Graham contended in *Changing Russia* (1913) that the moneyed Russian middle class treated its stomach like a god. The dining room (covered in wallpaper with, say, 'a frieze of grape tangles and dead partridges') was the most important room in the house.

Russia's socially critical intelligentsia saw things differently. In Chekhov's world, enjoying your food, as the unhappily married heroine's fat, smug and boring husband conspicuously does in *Anna Round the Neck* (1895), is a very bad sign. Conversely, a summer

1908 meal at the Gulf of Finland dacha of the painter Ilya Repin and his companion Natalya Nordman bitterly disappointed bon viveur Fyodor Fidler. Served on coarse pottery plates were 'borshch with almost no beetroot', 'meat patties that actually contained mainly bread', green peas and mashed potato, 'and of all things, raspberry ice-cream'. 'Not one drop' of drink was offered. Nordman became one of Russia's pioneering vegetarians. Like Leo Tolstoy, she argued publicly against meat-eating, but also wrote a pamphlet, pointedly entitled *A Cookbook for the Hungry*, that lent practical support to a streamlined and morally aware diet (1911).

In pre-1917 records, the lives of the less fortunate are glimpsable only at one remove. Literate peasants and workers were an advantaged minority, and any records they left convey the sense of their own good fortune. In his 1907 autobiography, Dimitry Kuznetsov, a student at a teacher training college run by the Holy Synod, concentrates on the high days of village life, weddings and festivals when 'the table groaned with things to eat'.[10]

In any case, experience evades generalization. Skilled workers settled in cities lived very different lives from recent migrants, but by the late nineteenth century, artels (worker cooperatives) and non-profit canteens were a lifeline for the latter too. Under serfdom, peasants working for their owners as domestic servants, or released by those owners on payment of obrok (an annual income tax), lived much more comfortably than those providing sweated labour on poor land. Emancipation in 1861 created distinctions between communities with larger landholdings on poor soil, and those with less land, but more favourable conditions. Even in European Russia, there were large regional and indeed local differences, as is clear from the enormous survey carried out in the late 1890s by the Ethnographical Bureau of Prince Vladimir Tenishev.[11] In some areas with significant out-migration, such as Yaroslavl Province, village communities had partly assimilated to urban ways. But poorer and richer families in the same area lived very different lives. Crop failure could push the whole community into crisis: 'There has been no famine here of late, and so no need for surrogate foods', wrote one of the survey's informants in 1899 (Kostroma Province).[12] It could have been very different.

The end of the old world

Once the country descended into world war, the gulf between the comfortably off and the precarious widened. Even at the Front, Mikhail Lemke noted on 15 February 1916, Nicholas II's chefs could whip up chicken soup, roast beef and profiteroles, accompanied by kvas and three wines (served in silver goblets to avoid breakages). However, soldiers were faced with food that was either monotonous (barley or rice soup) or (shades of *Battleship Potemkin*) disgusting: 'We had a small portion of beans for supper – more maggots in it, probably, than actual beans', NCO Nikolai Mursatov of the Kherson regiment remembered. As the conflict wore on, supplies dwindled and lines lengthened. 'Even black bread is short, let alone white', wrote Vladimir Telyakovsky, then in Yaroslavl, on 10 January 1917. In Petrograd during February 1917, unrest in the bread lines spilled into momentous political change.

One side-effect of revolution was to transform for ever the lives of the 'middle state', now known as 'former people'. As Countess Olga Sivers, the Russian owner of an estate in Ukraine's Poltava Province, complained on 9 October 1918:

> The whole of the last few days has gone on housekeeping: I made sauerkraut and salted cucumbers for the winter, which meant freezing for several hours in our primitive icehouse, to which one must descend down a ladder. I washed the cucumbers in boiled water and stood them in a barrel, scattered them with dill, horseradish, oak leaves, and then poured a brine over them. I had put into this brine saltpetre and sugar as well as salt, according to advice I had from various places, but no-one could give me any idea what the necessary quantities were. I have to do everything experimentally, and cannot tell what the results will be. In my sixth decade of life, I've had to learn how to do all these things.

Sivers was lucky in at least having the cucumbers to hand. Among city-dwellers, panic dashes to rural areas for produce were common.

In 'Free Passage' (September 1918), the poet Marina Tsvetaeva remembered a trip to Usman, 500 km from Moscow, and persuading reluctant peasant women to swap dress material, soap and matches for millet. At home, she and her daughters got by on potatoes boiled up in the samovar.[13] It was very different from the pre-revolutionary era, when cooks used a bottle of madeira where foreign ones would use a glass, and served fillet steak double the size of the 450 grams standard in France.

Yet some 'former people', provided they were useful to the new order, got favourable treatment. Worried by what would happen when his wartime rations ran out, literary scholar Nikolai Mendelson called the arrival in April 1920 of his 'professorial ration' (flour, herring, millet, sugar, salt, oil, butter, coffee, soap, matches and tobacco) 'a red-letter day'. Such initial beneficiaries often fared worse under the 'New Economic Policy' introduced in 1921, when social support was cut, and food prices rose. Many were reduced to looking wistfully through windows at the elaborate goods now available to the fortunate. For the refugees who fled Russia in the post-revolutionary years, economical living was also a way of life: a modest cuisine of soups, salads and stews became the norm, with more extravagant cooking reserved for major feasts.[14]

Plenty for some

Travelling to Yerevan in 1926, Marietta Shaginyan noted the delicious dumplings, buns and pies for sale in the 'rich villages' of south-eastern Russia. This reflected a time of relative prosperity for Russian peasants, absolute owners of their lands for the first time, and subject to progressive taxation, rather than requisitions. Forced collectivization, begun in 1929, brought the idyll to a catastrophic end. The epicentres of famine were Ukraine and Kazakhstan, but villagers starved in the Russian countryside also. Poor harvests and severe shortages (particularly of meat, as peasants slaughtered their own cows rather than collectivize them) brought privation to cities. Some had to sell treasured possessions through state stores that exchanged precious metals and other valuables for food coupons. 'Torgsin has gobbled everything in return for butter, sugar, porridge oats and millet', lamented Leningrader Sofya Ostrovskaya in July 1933. So little was available in ordinary shops, noted Una Pope-Hennessy, that people joked the letter M was about to be abolished – after all, there was no meat, milk or butter or oil (maslo), to be had.

All the same, life in the USSR's cities was infinitely more comfortable than conditions elsewhere. In January 1934, Varvara Malakhieva-Mirovich, living in a small town in Kaluga province, noted that only 'responsible officials' had electricity or paraffin. 'Ordinary clerks are half-starved; they live on meatless soup and boiled vegetables without butter or oil. Potatoes are sold in back streets on the sly […] Bread sales start at 3 a.m. and the swearing and shouting in the line has to be heard to be believed.' As an eighteen-year-old Siberian, Vasily Trushkin, recorded on 14 February 1940: 'There are huge bread lines everywhere in town and all you can get in the canteen is oatmeal soup and oat porridge.'

But also in 1934, Alexandra Kollontai, calling on her former Party Women's Section protégée, Polina Zhemchuzhina, the wife of Vyacheslav Molotov, one of Stalin's most trusted allies, complained, 'All these rich soups and meat dishes are just unhealthy.' By the end of the 1930s, food supplies for the Soviet elite in a broad sense – not just Party bosses but engineers, technicians, doctors, professors, and prominent writers and artists – were abundant. On 2 May 1940, Maria Vorobyova, a 34-year-old teacher from the Leningrad area, proud of her 'crêpe de Chine and silk georgette and shantung blouses' and 'elegant, fashionable shoes' (she hoped to save up for a squirrel coat and a piano), boasted to her diary: 'Dinner today is a plate of grapes, a spring onion omelette, blackcurrant kissel, a cup of coffee with a slice of buttercream gâteau. Not bad, eh? And, you know, I can dine like that every day.'

The reason why the years of the Great Purges were so often called 'a feast in time of plague' was that supplies were lavish – for the right people.[15] Explorers, at the symbolic heart of the culture, lived particularly cossetted lives, obsessively recording in their diaries the constituents of every meal. 'Three thousand chickens ended their earthly existence to go to the Pole in powdered form', enthused Ernst Krenkel on 1 June 1937. He was equally delighted with a rich layered gâteau, carefully tinned, accompanied by a message of obsequious congratulation from the factory craft worker who had made it.

The Soviet media celebrated the new availability of small luxuries. The Rostov-on-Don champagne factory was due to release 3 million bottles next year, *Pravda* reported on 18 March 1938. At the time, the population of Rostov was about half a million; for most, this was a New Year's Day drink, if that. Still, champagne was sometimes available even during the war.

Wartime food shortages were a taboo topic. However, publications in medical journals, and pamphlets on how to use surrogates, provided indirect testimony of their existence. *The Book of Tasty and Nutritious Food* was not republished until 1945, and then in altered form. It included numerous recipes for meatless dishes (for instance, 'meatballs' made of cabbage). Even in the 1948 edition, the range of meat soups had shrunk. But the edition of 1952 resembled more a colour catalogue of industrially produced foods than a conventional cookbook. It reflected the celebratory mood at the Nineteenth Congress of the Communist Party in October 1952, concluding the first phase of a drive to raise agricultural production during the post-war effort to rebuild the USSR.

(In)sufficiency for all

Under Stalin, inequity of provision was the rule. High officials could aspire to single-family flats; lesser mortals crammed rooms in former bourgeois apartments (or on the other hand, perched in wooden houses, still widespread even in bigger cities). The all-out building boom of the Khrushchev and Brezhnev years standardized accommodation; it also standardized the distribution of food. There was a push to raise output and efficiency, both through mechanization of production lines and by the employment of new ingredients. 'Chemistry into Life' was a mantra of the day, applied not just to disinfectant and furniture polish but to the use of flavourings that were 'identical to the natural ones' – and much cheaper to make. An example was vanillin, which made its way into millions of kitchens in little paper packets.[16]

With the abandonment of political terror as a means of controlling the population, Stalin's successors needed to pay more attention to public opinion. Rigid controls on public association and press censorship remained in place, but serious research on social attitudes became possible (for the first time since the late 1920s). Instead of inculcating gratitude in the population for the gifts cascaded from above, Soviet leaders now engaged explicitly, if clumsily, with consumer demand, highlighted in the First Seven-Year Plan of 1959 and the Food Supply Plan of 1982 and showcased in dozens of brochures and newspaper articles.

In the Stalin years, *The Book of Tasty and Nutritious Food* had boasted that food in the USSR was of world-beating quality. However, only a small minority got the chance to put the assertion to the test. Under Stalin's successors, buying ordinary produce became easier. Nikolai Kozakov, who spent 8 March 1962, a public holiday, in the provincial town of Arzamas, sarcastically observed: 'The dishes corresponded entirely to the era of fantastic abundance that has descended on sinful Russia from the tribunes of the Twenty-Second Party Congress: potato and beetroot salad, caviar made of semolina and onions, mushroom caviar (almost like the real thing, pressed), mushrooms, tomatoes, salted cabbage, cod in oil, boiled potatoes and dried flounder. In sum, the table was groaning with Khrushchev-era delicacies. Only sweetcorn was missing.'

The point, of course, was that none of these foods represented 'abundance', in Kozakov's view. Yet he was no member of the metropolitan elite, but a resident of the provinces – albeit with a well-paid profession (a chauffeur). As social conditions improved, expectations also rose, a process tragically clear in the protests against food price rises in Novocherkassk on 2 June 1962, suppressed by the military, police and KGB at the cost of twenty-four deaths. The following year, Khrushchev made the momentous decision to begin large-scale imports of grain from the United States. This was a sign of how vital to the social contract the provision of food at acceptable prices had become.

Hierarchies of supply endured into the new era – Moscow at the top, followed by Leningrad and the capitals of the republics, then down through cities large and small to rural areas. Direct distribution in the workplace took scarce goods to priority groups, and shops in prestigious places were better supplied. You could come back from Protvino, the home of a major particle physics research institute, with ten bottles of mayonnaise, when obtaining even one was usually a problem.[17] Provincial visitors to the Kremlin took care to cram their briefcases with the delicacies available in the buffets of the country's political nerve centre.

As Anatoly Naiman and Galina Narinskaya recalled in their 2003 essay 'Food and Conversation', beyond the Kremlin, what you could buy was limited:

> It amounted to a dozen or so foods, two dozen at most. Butter, cooking oil, eggs, sausage, potatoes, herring, chicken with blue goosepimples, frozen hake, Polish or Egyptian onions, bottled green peas (unless you missed the one day in the year, between 10 and 15 September, when they were actually on sale for a whole hour), curd cheese in a chocolate coat, pasteurised milk, Buratino caramels.

All the items mentioned were classic examples of 'defitsit', goods that were snapped up in quantity because they appeared on sale irregularly – a practice that meant they instantly disappeared from sale. By the 1980s, even some large cities (e.g. Voronezh) had seasonal shortages (of potatoes, for instance), others rationing for key goods (e.g. Perm), while in others again (e.g. Ufa), people depended entirely on private exchanges to buy food at all.

When it came to packaging, shop staff displayed virtuosic skills, turning sugar-paper into tightly wrapped parcels despite the lack of string or tape (similar was the speed of their mental arithmetic, and fingers on abacuses to tot up the bill). But you needed your own bottles, jars and boxes. The famous avoska (ever-expandable string bag) was only the start. No wonder that in retrospect, people recall buying food as an activity requiring guile, persistence and savvy. By the 1960s, though, consumption of basic foods had reached world averages for developed countries, and in 1989, milk, eggs, fish and sugar consumption levels were higher than in the United States. For the first time in Russian history, dying of starvation was not a threat. Yet those who felt gratitude were the least advantaged and the least visible: older members of the rural population.

Farm to table

Before 1917, food manufacture, like food marketing, was overwhelmingly artisanal: from home-made goods taken to market and kitchens in the back of small shops up to factories with perhaps 50–100 employees at most. To twenty-first-century ears, this sounds attractive: small-producer meat, milk and vegetables, prepared with integrity. However, sources from the period itself rudely disrupt such a pastoral vision. Hazards such as ergot (a fungus with potentially fatal neurotoxic effects) in grain crops, particularly rye, and brucellosis and TB in milk were ever-present. If produce got to the market in good shape, it did not necessarily reach consumers that way. 'Foodstuffs in household use have never been so insolently falsified as in our time', wrote Mariya Redelin in 1900. Mouldy wheat, milk adulterated with water, flour, starch or chalk, 'butter' comprised mixed fats and potato, and cheese with lentil flour, were just some of the occupational hazards. And that was before one came to the more 'innocent' cases of food that was contaminated, putrid or simply of poor quality.

It was such laissez-faire that Soviet leaders sought to combat by the imposition of state control. In theory, state farms and state factories meant quality for everyone. But if the failings of Tsarist-era food production often derived from the absence of state intervention, Soviet food production was bedevilled by its excess. From 1928 onwards, central planning imposed USSR-wide targets for key food products, leading to an emphasis on resource extraction that had high human as well as ecological costs. Workers on collective and state farms began receiving wages, as opposed to a share of the farm's returns, only in 1966. Most inhabitants of the Soviet countryside were tied to their home village until 1974, when they were finally allowed access to the nationwide 'internal passport' system. Upbeat propaganda such as posters of Pasha Angelina, the pioneering woman tractor-driver, or footage in Ivan Pyryev's *The Cossacks of the Kuban* (1950), showing tables loaded with food, belied a reality of sweated labour. As the country recovered after the war, widowed peasant women often pulled the plough themselves. In the late Soviet period, conditions improved significantly, with guaranteed prices for produce, but flight to the cities accelerated, and underinvestment and low productivity remained endemic. Staying in the village increasingly signified social failure.

Wages in food production were also low, and the sector had a high percentage of women, always a sign of low prestige. Some factories enjoyed high repute (for instance, the former von Einem chocolate works). Conditions in others were primitive. Under pressure to comply with targets, staff might turn a blind eye to quality or even hygiene. But every so often, offenders were noisily punished. State control also allowed redress to the determined consumer, who could complain directly to a shop, write to the municipal or Party authorities, or send an indignant letter to the press. Such recourses were, however, one of the ways in which Soviet culture in fact benefitted less the socially oppressed in whose name the country had been created than the heirs of the advantaged classes who had been the targets of 'class war'.

In the home kitchen

Whether getting food on the table was a necessity or a pleasure was constrained not just by the food you could buy but also by the time you had to spare. Before the Revolution, most families even from the 'middle state' were able to rely on the services of a professional, whether a (female) 'plain cook' or the more ambitious (male) 'chef'. But after 1917, housework became the responsibility of the individual family – above all, its female members.

True, from the 1920s to the 1960s, the more privileged professional families often had 'house workers', a Soviet euphemism for what would have been called 'a cook-general' in contemporary Britain or America. But these were usually young women, fresh from the village (in Boris Barnet's comic film, *The House on Trubnaya Square*, one arrives clutching her duck). Expecting them to produce chicken in aspic or pikeperch with hollandaise sauce would have been futile. Now, such dishes were left to restaurants and high-end caterers.

In the early 1960s, widening opportunities for factory work dried up the supply of villagers using domestic service to settle in the cities. Labour-saving was the watchword. Natalya Baranskaya's story *A Week Like Any Other* (1969) showed women scientists rushing to the shops during part of the lunchbreak and scooping up sausage, milk, butter, processed cheese and minced meat patties, all to be turned into quick, if uninspiring, meals. Vladimir Menshov's massively popular film *Moscow Doesn't Believe in Tears* (1979) drew a moralizing contrast between the supermarket jars and packets that the affluent but lonely heroine put on the table, and the communal celebrations of friends who had stayed in the working class. The appropriate medicine for social ills was home-made food. Exactly how much time and effort that cost was a question that fell into silence.

Still, despite the pressures, home cooking became more adventurous from the 1960s on, helped partly by a diversifying specialist cookbook market. If the *Book of Tasty and Nutritious Food* was a dream factory, the new-style cookbooks were more practical: drab manuals printed on yellow paper, with cramped line illustrations at most. But new types of cookery guidance were also starting to emerge. William Pokhlyobkin first came to public attention as a columnist for *Nedelya* (*This Week*), the Saturday supplement to *Izvestiya*, a landmark of Soviet human-interest journalism from the Khrushchev era onwards. *Nedelya* mixed features with 'state of the nation' commentaries – grandmothers as carers, sex education for adolescents. Advice on everyday life also took up a good deal of room, and it was here that Pokhlyobkin's cookery columns came in.

Pokhlyobkin's articles, and later books, were, in the Soviet context, radically new. Here was an identifiable real-life author, unlike the faceless committees responsible for most earlier cookery books – and one with a name so weird that it sounded like a pseudonym ('Mr

Souper'). To boot, Pokhlyobkin was a food *writer*, not only, or indeed mainly, the purveyor of recipes. In a sense, he was a Soviet version of Elizabeth David, who in early editions of *Italian Food* (1954) recommended Primula processed cheese to replace unavailable soft cheeses such as Bel Paese, or M. F. K. Fisher, whose *How to Cook a Wolf* encouraged her readers to make exotic dishes from tins. While Pokhlyobkin, the citizen of a country with closed borders, lacked the opportunities to travel that gave David and Fisher cachet, he made imaginary voyages, roaming back into the Russian past and to far-flung countries, courtesy of his library.

Still more important than expanding advice was 'technology transfer'. This was not so much a question of labour-saving devices (though by the late Soviet period, some families did have, say, an electric 'mikser' at their disposal). It related to something more fundamental: the cooker itself. In the early nineteenth century, the traditional wood-fired 'Russian stove' began giving way, in city households, to 'modern' ranges, allowing greater control over temperature. After 1917, though, firewood shortages meant stoves and ranges were only fired for special occasions. The everyday resource was a paraffin-fired primus stove. As a result, frying, boiling and stewing were the methods, unless you happened to have a 'wonder pot', a stacked aluminium saucepan that produced a passable imitation of oven-baked food.[18]

For most people, the arrival of modern cookers went in step with mains gas (unavailable in most places before the late 1950s at earliest; electric cookers took another couple of decades). Out of habit, people mainly used the hob rather than the oven, and grilling was still reserved for outdoors. But even so, the provision of steady, easily regulated heat represented a major change, plus the fact that you could cook different dishes simultaneously. Even in communal apartments, tenants could abandon the primus.

Resources for storage had also improved significantly, at least compared with the recent past. Traditional Russian domestic space always included reserves for putting food by: a secure, temperature-stable cellar, an icehouse or at the very least, a walk-in larder. In Soviet 'communal apartments', or student or factory hostels, food could not safely be left in the kitchen. This left the space between your room's double windows as a rudimentary chiller, and ordinary cupboards (sometimes shared with clothes) for dry goods.

Only on city peripheries (and in small towns and the countryside) were traditional storage systems maintained. This made a significant difference in times of scarcity. On 22 December 1941, when most of the population was living on watery soup and adulterated bread, Natalya Panchenko and her mother made the 'enormous journey', on foot through transportless Leningrad, at risk of air-raids and shellfire, to see friends out in Ozerki, 12 km north of Nevsky prospekt. 'For breakfast they gave us a saucer of noodles and a saucer of buckwheat gruel, two glasses of sweet coffee with milk and a slice of bread. Dinner was a plate of thick soup with millet and salted tomatoes, then rye noodles with meat and a cup of compote, and more bread. God above! It's been an age since we ate like that.' Most people in central Leningrad, without the capacity to salt vegetables and meat and store grain, to bake their own bread, or even to make jam, lived, at longest, on a three- to four-day cycle. As he recalled in his memoirs, Dmitry Likhachev and his wife Vera were unusual in storing even dry bread, potatoes, fish oil and vitamin C tablets. Having such stores was so rare that it could be interpreted as 'hoarding' and seen as justification for theft.

The modern single-family apartments of the late twentieth century did have built-in storage: 'ceiling space' that could be used for jars and bottles, and sometimes a so-called 'cold cupboard' set into the kitchen's outside wall. In the most fortunate cases, built-in cupboards were supplied. The Khrushchev years also saw an upsurge in refrigerator production. The memorial apartment of Sergei Kirov, Leningrad's Party leader from 1926 to 1934, houses a gleaming American icebox that was, at the time, the only one in the entire city. Soviet-made fridges began rolling off the production lines in the late 1940s, but reached only a selected few (just over 6000 model ZIS were released in 1956). In the late 1950s, output rates rose dramatically, and production of the compact Saratov line had reached over a million by the early 1960s.

Over the next three decades, a substantial fridge, with freezer compartments, became the 'best friend' of more and more cooks.

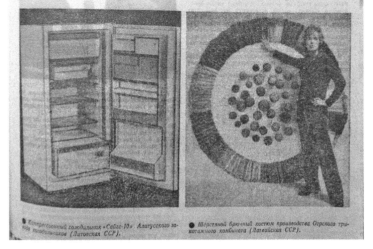

ТОВАРЫ ДЛЯ ВСЕХ — ДЕЛО ВСЕХ!

Производство новых товаров, красивых, удобных, практичных,— одна из главных задач, которую поставил XXIV съезд КПСС и которая должна быть решена в девятой пятилетке.

Что для этого нужно сделать, на какие изделия обратить особое внимание, кто отвечает за выпуск новой и совершенствование уже освоенной продукции — об этом говорится в постановлении ЦК КПСС и Совета Министров СССР «О мерах по обеспечению дальнейшего развития производства товаров массового спроса».

К празднику мы делаем друг другу подарки. Вещи, которые вы видите здесь на фотографиях,— подарки всем нам. Это лишь очень малая часть тех новых товаров, которые скоро появятся на прилавках магазинов. Их будет становиться с каждым днем все больше, а главное — они будут все лучше и доступнее.

● Магнитофон «Электрон-302» — новинка Московского приборного завода.

● Компрессионный холодильник «Саба-10» Алитусского завода холодильников (Литовская ССР).

● Шерстяной брючный костюм производства Огрского трикотажного комбината (Латвийская ССР).

Figure 0.2 Goods for Everyone Is Everyone's Business! *Nedelya*, 1971.

(see Figure 0.2). Those buying for large families sometimes had two. Even students might have fridges in their shared rooms, rented by the month, and the better class of hotels uniformly provided them to guests (this helpful custom endured into the post-Soviet era also). As dachas, or summer residences, became commoner in Soviet families, so they likewise began to serve the storage economy. Mothers, grandmothers and aunts filled endless bottles with jams and pickled or fermented vegetables. 'Empty shops, but full fridges', ran a joking paradox of the day.

The culinary repertoire

When people are faced with the practicalities of putting food on the table, ideological considerations subside. Ekaterina Avdeeva's boast that she had filled *Handbook of the Experienced Russian Housewife* with dishes reflecting the *Russian* 'locality, climate, and way of life' did not stop her from including recipes with lemons and olives. Yet culinary tradition sometimes exercised real force. Take the meal served in 1808 to Stepan Zhikharev by a Moscow gentleman, 'the very prototype of a top civil servant of the old school':

> There were cabbage soup with dough twists, kasha with chopped eggs and bone marrow [...] a huge poached bream garnished with vegetables and horseradish, sausages with fat green peas, a joint of remarkably tender and juicy roast veal with cucumbers, and finely, a round pie of coarse flour filled with jam as dessert.

Comparable dishes are listed in the sixteenth-century domestic manual, the *Domostroi*. The 1808 menu also captures various long-term characteristics of the Russian kitchen: the preference for soft textures over chewy or crisp, the joy in rich pastries and meats, the liking for sharp or tart tastes to offset all the fats, the affection for some strong tastes (vinegar, horseradish, mustard, dill and caraway) combined with suspicion of others. As the sixteenth-century household manual, *Domostroi*, makes clear, medieval Russians enjoyed saffron, cinnamon, cloves, ginger and nutmeg. But the role of spices in the nineteenth- and twentieth-century Russian kitchen was more limited, and the word used for hot peppers, *gorkii*, was also used to mean 'bitter' – not in a complimentary way.

However authentic in objective terms, the meal Zhikharev was served up was also a bluff, self-defining gesture – just like the host's declaration that he did not propose to serve the diners the new-fangled drink of coffee. Equally polemical was the title of Nikolai Osipov's *The Old-Time Russian Housewife, Housekeeper and Cook* (1794), which included dishes similar to those Zhikharev ate – ham, onion and cabbage soup; beetroot with vinegar and horseradish; and a round pie.

To insist on culinary tradition is to acknowledge by negation the existence of dishes that compatriots (unwisely, of course) choose to enjoy. Despite the sallies of patriots, large numbers of foreign foods and techniques became widespread among those who could afford them. This included the grandees with their menus in French and repertoire of emulsified sauces, truffled grouse in aspic and bombes surprises. But it also included more modest menus. In the writings of Dr Puf, for instance, hachis, velouté sauce and beurre noir sat alongside mince pies, sage-and-onion stuffing (tactfully presented as 'apothecary's duck'), bread sauce, cayenne pepper and bottled condiments such as 'Caboul sauce' (something like modern Worcester or HP). Odoevsky's occasional liking for food served very plainly, 'without dressing', was also very English.

It was not just food from beyond the borders that made its way into Russian diets. Over the nineteenth and twentieth centuries, dishes from the further reaches of empire started to become ensconced in the Russian kitchen. A famous example was 'Little Russian' (Ukrainian) borshch, listed by Ekaterina Avdeeva's *Handbook* among other dishes that had 'come into use among Russians': Polish zrazy (stuffed beef roulade) and kurnik (chicken pie), Ukrainian varenyky (dough parcels) and Lithuanian kolduny dumplings.

All these were dishes from the Western reaches of the Russian Empire, where cultural traditions were similar. In Ukraine particularly, a Russian-speaking elite aspired to 'Great Russian', rather than 'Little Russian', values, to use the patronizing terminology of the time, but often spoke Ukrainian and espoused local traditions too.[19] Russians from comparable social groups took an interest in the food of the eastern reaches also, but were less ready to assimilate it. In Derzhavin's *Felitsa*, plov or pilaff supplies a note of Oriental luxury, like the silk robes of the grandee enjoying it. Vasily Zhukovsky recorded in his diary eating Crimean Tatar dishes such as sarma börek (cheese pie) and spiced çorba soup, but made no comment on the taste; he used the names for local colour, as he did the names of his hosts. Boris Volzhin's 1842 *Encyclopaedia* supplied three recipes for plov – Turkish, Venetian and Stamboul – all with an exotic ring.

Soviet culture was likewise shaped by a mixture of foreign and imperial influences. Anastas Mikoyan, the minister in charge of the food industry between 1934 and 1938, came back from a 1936 trip to the United States with an admiration not just for bottled mayonnaise but for frankfurters, automatic restaurants and ice cream. The 1939 version of *The Book of Tasty and Nutritious Food* recommended chicory, more a staple of French shops than Soviet ones. But Russian cuisine bourgeoise was not forgotten: the book also had a section of recipes 'from old cookbooks', including an 1847 veal ragout and a 1790 dish of mushrooms. There were some surreptitious borrowings from Molokhovets as well, particularly dishes in aspic. As for the wider empire, the spotlight was on Georgian food (predictably, given Stalin's nationality), and mainly on its less 'exotic' dishes (roast meat in Georgian wine, say). However, in later years, dishes from other parts of the empire, including Armenian bozbash (lamb soup), began to figure also. The 1964 edition of the *Book of Tasty and Nutritious Food* showcased an unlikely solyanka (a thoroughly Russian soup of brined pickles and meat) 'in the Georgian style'.

Rather slower to get a place on the Russian table, in however adapted a form, were dishes from Central Asia. This was partly because the conquest of these territories began only in the 1860s, and partly because the original Russian populations were small and mingled to a limited extent with 'the natives' (in 1897, Tashkent had just over 14,000 Russians, with their own city quarter, in a population of 137,000). But during the early Soviet period, the quintessentially colonial influx of 'special settlers' was joined by waves of new migrants, no longer automatically superior on grounds of nationality. By 1970, the proportion of Russians in Tashkent had reached 40 per cent.

Old-style colonial superiority was challenged by the national policies of the 1920s, aimed at the creation of local cadres. It was also undermined by the contrast between the abundance in Central Asia and what you could get in Russia itself. Nina Pokrovskaya, who lived in Uzbekistan from 1921 to 1930, recalled in a diary entry for 30 September 1930 how 'mountains of fruit, white loaves, flatbreads, plov, kebabs, lamb astonished us after the starving Volga region'. On a return visit to Central Asia in 1956, Pokrovskaya eyed with a mixture of distaste and fascination the behaviour of an assimilated Russian acquaintance: 'He casts off the heavy burden of civilisation and happens into his usual well-worn striped Uzbek robe and cap and his battered slippers and, sprawling on the carpet and practically belching with joy, crams plov with both hands straight into his mouth.' All the same, she herself deeply regretted the sterile, Sovietized landscape of Tashkent. Uzbek culture was to be relished – with discretion.

Confronted with, say, the 'superstitious' attachment to amulets, Russian visitors tended to feel superior. Central Asian food, though, inspired wonder mixed with inadequacy. As historian Vladimir Bessonov enthused on a visit to Taraz (then Dzhambul) in September 1982:

> Your eyes are on stalks: a woman peeling carrots with a vast knife, doing something else with them, scattering pepper and salt – it's so delicious, your mouth starts watering. And here are the vegetable rows: marrows, mountains of onions, every kind of herb – kinza [green coriander], mint, dill, ginger, cardamom, herbs whose name I don't even know; through the kebab smoke, you can see mountains of tomatoes the size of two fists; in copper basins, chebureki [dough parcels with meat] are sizzling in fat [...] And on and on the bazaar goes, and it's so pleasant to walk down the long counters, fixing your eyes now on salted cucumbers, now on juicy pomegranates cut open in a star of seeds. What won't you find! And then, just a little way away, you come to the state farm stall with its potatoes, where someone is shovelling them into bags from the filthy heap with an ill-formed spade. The 'merits' of the collective farm system are plain to see.

The first edition of *Kulinariya* (1955), mainly intended as a restaurant manual, had a whole section of 'dishes of the peoples of the republics'. 'Soviet cuisine', opined the Introduction, 'is made up of dishes generally in use with us; it is adorned to an equal extent with Russian pies, and Ukrainian borshch, and Uzbek plov, Georgian shashlik, Armenian tolma [dolma], Azerbaijani pitta, and many other superb dishes and appetisers of all the peoples of our country' (see Figure 0.3).

Figure 0.3 Empire at table: kebabs, lavash flatbreads, fruit, mineral water and wine from the Caucasus as well as Russian pickles and chopped salad (*Kulinariya*, 1955).

By the end of the 1950s, plov was indeed to a strong degree naturalized. In his diaries from then (and until the 1980s), scientist Oleg Amitrov regularly noted it as a party dish among his friends. A grey, greasy and gristly version was even for sale in the buffet next to the rooms where we had Russian lessons at Hostel No. 4 in Voronezh.

The small-scale adoption before 1917 of specialities and ingredients from non-Russian parts of the empire (Polish truffles, say, or Ukrainian cucumbers) contrasted with the emergence of a truly 'imperial' cuisine in the late twentieth century. But Sovietization also worked in reverse. A dispiriting guesthouse close to Lake Sevan in Armenia served delegates of a 1985 scientific conference 'buckwheat kasha with tinned stew'. They only tasted the lake's famous fish, along with lavash flatbreads, local cheese, bunches of green herbs and grilled lamb, at an impromptu picnic organized by the convenors.[20] As Russian-Soviet tastes rippled outwards, even former reindeer herders in the far north-east of the USSR began growing cucumbers and watermelons.[21]

Certainly, homogenization had its limits. Maize meal had been widely eaten in Ukraine, Moldova and parts of the Caucasus since at least the late seventeenth century. But Khrushchev's attempts to popularize it in Russia made the leader a figure of fun. 'I'd go with Khrushchev double quick', ran one scabrous ditty, 'but they say he's got corn where he should have a dick'. All the same, just as central Asians took to pork, vodka and tomatoes, Russians began making pies with Uzbek dried apricots and using spicy Georgian ajika and sour green-plum tkemali sauce as relishes. In the early twenty-first century, you could get a dozen different kinds of rice in Russian supermarkets, and it was as easy to find the Georgian spice mix khmeli-suneli as garam masala in Britain.

As new dishes arrived, others quietly vanished. Some dishes still present on the modern table – fish soup, for instance – go back to the *Domostroi*. But the fact that lamb appears first in the *Domostroi*'s list of meats would surprise modern Russian cooks, still more a dish mixing pluck and grain like the Scottish haggis and the Swedish lungmos or pölsa. The sheep's intestines stuffed with egg also mentioned by the *Domostroi* would not have fazed early nineteenth-century Russian cooks (they appear, for instance, in Boris Volzhin's 1842 domestic encyclopaedia). They would seem peculiar now. On the other hand, 'omlet' is homely as bread.

It is precisely these borrowings that give Russian food its character. Many dishes with a long history (dark breads and pancakes, cooked grain porridges, pickled and brined vegetables, fish, thick soups, roast meat and game, mushrooms, fruit syrups and jams) are widespread in the Nordic and Baltic countries, and many can be found in the traditional Scottish diet too. There is an equally wide northern European distribution of the ingredients that seem most 'alien' to southern Europeans, and indeed some English or American observers (sour cream, beetroot, berries, caraway seeds, dill). But in Russia, as in Britain and the Netherlands, the north European culinary practices modulated, as the empire developed, into a culinary hybrid.

Going global

Even in the Brezhnev era, Russian food was not nearly as monotonous as the Naimans's list of standard products would have suggested. A family feast might have comprised Georgian cheese pies as well as pickled vegetables and a chopped salad, with fried potatoes, but also spatchcocked chicken tabaka.

In public catering, manuals with recipes for 200 portions of Pozharsky chicken cutlets or potato and beetroot salad, each to weigh 120 and 140 grams respectively, made for dull results. Yet inconsistency was also a fact of life. While the 'state quality standard' in theory ensured uniformity of output, the rules were quite liberal as to substitutions.[22] It took inside knowledge to work out which of several identical-looking dishes tasted better than the others, even if none of them was likely actually to give you food poisoning.

With the disappearance of the Soviet Union, standardization also disappeared. Even under perestroika, public catering had started to change, since the service sector was one of the areas where so-called 'cooperatives' (private businesses run under the notional control of the Komsomol) were allowed to operate. Their impact was often bizarre. I remember a trip round the Moscow Arbat, in snowy mid-December 1988, where our pitstops took in a lurid orange soft drink, paired with shortbread biscuits, then, after a lengthy search, pork kebabs that, when we bit into them, turned out to be as rare as roast beef. By then we were so hungry that we ate them with relish (and fortunately, without ill effects). 'Don't buy anything on the street', friends belatedly warned us. But indoor venues also had their hazards: in one major Moscow library, a tribe of cats commuted between the lavatories and the canteen.

Eating at home was not straightforward either. By 1990, food shortages escalated to levels unseen for decades. With the removal of market controls in 1992, prices on basic products surged. This was the era when someone could decide to buy a bottle of oil on the way back from work, only to find, when they left the office, that they could no longer afford it.

Once the situation stabilized, the consumer was confronted with a bewildering array of choices. Food imports flooded the market. Some reliable staples effectively disappeared, while others continued to exist in altered form. McDonalds was only the first and biggest foreign chain to raise its flag. New-style Russian eateries also proliferated, from pillared halls claiming to revive pre-revolutionary traditions to street booths. By the 2000s, canteens of the traditional kind persisted mainly in places frequented by elderly people, such as major public libraries. Sometimes old standards such as 'meat in a clay pot', with vastly improved supply lines, turned out to be delicious. But the overall market tendencies were very different: fast food (hamburgers, baked potatoes, filled pancakes); reasonably priced but limited café menus; 'family restaurants', often brasserie-style places with French-Italian offerings.

The 'local' had a rather limited foothold. Certainly, a few farm-to-table places made a name. But high-end 'auteur restaurants' were usually one or another variation of global.[23] However, by the late 2010s there were signs that some younger cooks were starting to offer, astutely, a kind of Russian or Siberian spin on the craze for foraged, Scandi-style food, and to adapt heritage cooking of the kind passed down in family manuscript books with new twists of their own. Ambitious home cooks followed in their wake.

Yet for many, particularly the old, market deregulation came as a huge shock. Restaurants and even cafés were out of reach for many pensioners. Supermarket chains made immense profits for their owners, but this meant high prices for customers. In central areas of cities, kiosks and small shops were squeezed out. Rather than obtaining fixed-price staples close to their homes, those short of money had to travel to 'people's shops' or markets in outlying areas.

When it came to the goods themselves, knowledge that people had acquired over years – that factory X produced quality milk products, while factory Y did not – was suddenly redundant. You now had to discriminate between a dozen different types of yoghourt, all differently priced, some with Western brand names, some Russian (though the ownership of the manufacturing company might have nothing to do with its flag of convenience). After 2014, use of non-milk fats (particularly palm oil) became so widespread that premium outlets made a feature of unadulterated milk. The new world was not a place simply of opportunity but of anxiety and indeed deprivation. Deficit lived on, even if now its cause was the sum at the bottom of the till receipt, rather than gaps in the contents of the chiller cabinet.

The internet was full of retro photograph pages and social website posts celebrating the wonders of Soviet food back in the days when state quality codes supposedly kept standards high.[24] All the same, there was often a distinction between what people said and what they did. What people saw as authentic could mean the supposed 'naturalness' of factory-produced Soviet food, or traditions of food production and preparation pre-dating the era of crash industrialization, mass catering and the standardization of cuisine. And it could also refer to Russian versions of international trends. In real life, as opposed to internet fantasy, it was not unknown to have gefilte fish served alongside sliced

Figure 0.4 Russian doll (matreshka) with three traditional food traders: butcher, milkmaid and fishwife. 1990s. Author's collection.

ham, which might come (at least supposedly) from Parma. There was a strong argument for seeing sushi, around since the 1990s, as a 'Russian' dish; certainly, it did not much resemble what is served in Japan under that name.

Food sanctions in the 2010s and 2020s had little impact; you could still get chorizo or Edam-style cheese, only now made in a local factory. Yet there were also eating places that specialized in 'authentic Russian' food: hearty soups, thick stews with potatoes, pies and buns, roast meats, to be supped with Khokhloma painted wooden spoons off style russe ceramics – hallowed traditions that had never quite existed in real life (see Figure 0.4).

Eating on the hop

Along with flexibility of food choices went a move away from formal menus into amorphous eating. The convention of moving from soup through fish, meat and then a sweet dish followed by dessert (nuts and fruit) with wine, or tea, cakes and jam, was known as *style russe* and, if not invented there, was certainly the accepted norm from the late eighteenth century onwards. But over time, anarchy crept in.

Soviet public catering offered 'all-in' lunches of salad, soup, main course and stewed fruit. However, family eating was less rigid. Having eaten, if they could, a solid breakfast, people would snack as they needed (perhaps a sandwich to avoid light-headedness or some cake during the tea- and coffee-drinking sessions that punctuated the working day). They would eat more substantially at 'dinner', a meal scheduled, as convenient, at any time from 12.00 to 5.00 pm or even later.

One could call this 'grazing', except that eating anywhere but a table tended to be frowned on. The commonest word for a party, 'zastolye', directly associated the furniture with the event: the fun was to be had sitting down. (Russian buffets, on the other hand, tended to be awkward affairs, either under-catered, or the reverse.) But if the table was essential to 'proper' eating, what was put on it was very varied. To adapt Mary Douglas: 'Between breakfast and the last nightcap, the food of the day does *not* come in an ordered pattern'.[25]

Adventitious eating became more widespread as food shortages worsened in the 1980s. You rarely passed up an opportunity to munch something that was at least 'edible': there was no telling when the next chance would come along. So, during the daytime, you snatched an ice cream (of reliable quality) to avoid a hunger faint, then later, out visiting, swallowed three evening meals in a row.

The flexible schedules and readiness to grab what you could persisted well after Soviet-era shortages had gone. For Sergei Esin, head of the Institute of Literature in Moscow, 3 October 2006 began with a tomato, bean and onion stew and millet kasha, then a slice of a pizza presented by a student's grandmother in a misguided effort to influence her marks. The day continued with a reception at the German Embassy ('they feed you better than anywhere else in Moscow') with Bratwurst, Leberkäse meatloaf and roasted ham hock (Schweinshaxe). Two portions of cream pudding with pear rounded off that meal. Esin's culinary tour then segued through lentils and onion fried in butter and a hefty hunk of poppy seed cake at a friend's, culminating with his return home at 10.00 pm for two 'juicy slices of watermelon'. On the other hand, a student or pensioner diary in the same year might have run from late breakfast of tea and fried eggs at 11.00 to a quick sandwich or square of chocolate with coffee at 4.00 pm and then evening tea with macaroni at 8.00 or 9.00. Slender beauties might skip lunch altogether, saving their calories for cake and cappuccino.

'Soup from an axe'

The dish that gives the strongest sense of the sheer variety of eating practices in Russia is soup. The basic concept of a solid-liquid mix boiled or poached together was captured by many different words: the modern standard term, *sup*, originally a genteelism of foreign origin; 'shchi' or 'shti', which goes back to the medieval period in the meaning 'fermented cabbage', but in the last couple of centuries, has tended to mean a meat and cabbage soup of the kind widespread in European peasant culture; 'pokhlyobka', which William Pokhlyobkin ordered, should be used only for light vegetable broths, but which disobedient laypersons regularly apply to thick meat ones; boltushka, a kind of gruel whipped up from flour or meal and water.

Soup was, in fact, the most basic *dish* as such. It had a special place in subsistence and shortage cooking, because it could be made from anything available. The old folk tale of a passing soldier who promised to show an old woman to make 'soup from an axe', and persuaded her to add 'just a little bit of onion and carrot' and then 'meat and barley' for flavour, illustrated not just soldiers' reputation for sharp practice but how ingredients were added as they became available.

Soups ran the entire culinary gamut: from the oyster bisque recommended by Dr Puf, or the hazel hen decoction served to Moscow gourmet Aleksei Ovchinnikov in 1919, through the cabbage and meat broths at family meals (better-off working-class families included), down to the watery brews, filling but not sustaining, thrown together during periods of famine. Soup was a staple of institutional cuisine, recognized as appropriate food for the needy back in the 1800s. It figured not just in 'soup kitchens' but in orphanages, schools and hospitals: it was a classic invalid food. At home, it was failsafe comfort eating for husbands and latchkey children to heat up, or to concoct themselves from leftovers.

Soup and state projects went hand in hand. During the 1810s, according to Fabian Gottlieb von Bellingshausen, Russian Polar explorers ventured forth with tinned bouillon from Donkin of London. In the Stalin era, they took specially produced packets for instant reconstitution. Some instant soup mixes were also staples of the civilian world: pea soup, along with brews of nutritional yeast, sustained Leningraders over the early months of 1942. Later pea soup became a fixture on canteen menus; filling but dreary.

By the time I first reached the USSR in 1979, soup generally was often a disappointment of public catering. 'Pickle soup' (rassolnik) would be made from leftover scraps rather than the traditional kidney, with gouts of grease and specks of unfiltered scum. Even less appetizing was 'milk soup', tepid and topped with skin, the nightmare of small children in nursery canteens, and of visiting foreign students.

These efforts were a travesty of the time-honoured ideal: soup so thick and rich the spoon could stand up in it. The contempt of some

Russian gastronomes for foreign food as unappetising and skimpy reached its apogee when confronted with, say, a Tuscan brew that tasted 'as though a passing chicken had dipped its leg in it'.[26] Generous amounts of meat or fish were essential to approval: soup without was known as 'empty', or, in the pre-revolutionary army, as 'shrapnel'. For the nineteenth century 'middle state', soup was the resonant opening course of the meal. In the twentieth, it often became, for better or worse, a dish on its own.

Improvised feasts

The flexibility of eating is poorly recognized by Russian cookbooks published in the West. To begin with, these often favour 'authentic' dishes, with less attention to eating practices at the time when they are written. Added to this the selection of dishes is often forced into the straitjacket of the traditional formal meal: starters, soups, main courses, vegetables and side dishes, puddings. The result is an order that bears little relation to the presentation of those dishes in Russia itself, whether now or in the past.

A case in point is 'zakuski', often translated as 'appetisers' or 'starters'. But the fundamental meaning of the word is closer to 'snack', particularly one served with drinks (above all vodka). The 'snacks' in question may range from a mere piece of bread (only sniffed, in the case of desperate alcoholics) to an integrated selection of varied dishes that resembles a Scandinavian smorgasbord. In the sybaritic belle époque, they turned into a grandiose spread served in a separate room, but more typical was Stepan Zhikharev's host in 1808, serving 'splendid caviar' and salmon with herb and galangal vodka. Zakuski can be less than an 'appetiser', but also a whole lot more.

Eating in Russia is strongly subject to improvisation, as a result both of external pressures and of emotional preferences (spontaneity and impulsiveness are valued). Dishes may pop up in all kinds of places. A chopped salad would now be a classic constituent of zakuski (partly because of its status as a starter in Soviet-era catering). But it could and can also be eaten as a meal on its own. Egg dishes and curd cheese patties are classic breakfast dishes, but widely consumed at other times; soup is a dinner special, but a Russian hotel's breakfast buffet normally includes a tureen or two, partly, no doubt, because of its efficiency as a hangover cure. Usually, sweet dishes follow savoury ones, but in 2018, I attended a diplomatic reception where guests demolished the entire table of desserts long before the first trays of meat stew limped in.

This flexibility means that cookbooks in Russia have tended to group recipes by dish – pies, stews, roasts, puddings. But pursuing the history of dishes as such is tricky, given that the same name can be applied to different things, and different names to the same.[27] It makes more sense to focus on the Russian kitchen's most highly favoured ingredients – grain; meat and milk products; game, foraged berries and mushrooms; fish; vegetables and plants; sweet dishes – and to trace the way in which they have been produced and prepared over the different eras.

Constants in the history of Russian food include the challenges of producing food in the teeth of harsh climatic conditions and of transporting it long-distance; the reliance of large cities on the rural hinterland; and resource extraction as one face of imperial rule, and dialogue with non-Russian cultures as another. But the last 200 years have also seen momentous changes. The move of the population from the country to the town transformed the population's relationship with some foods, notably bread, milk and meat, a process accelerated by the Soviet government's commitment to modernization. Even here, though, it was less a question of radically new things to eat (along the lines of plant- or insect-based protein in the 2020s) than of familiar foods in new forms. And in the case of game, or mushrooms and berries, state-sponsored reforms had negligible effects. By looking closely at individual foods, we can see how the 'history' of Russian food is made up of many different 'histories' and how what people ate was not just a question of state campaigns and expert advice. And we can also sense the ways in which food was won, in the face of an adverse climate, from the field and meadow, moor, river, sea and forest, and grasp how it was turned, by human labour, into dishes set upon the table.

CHAPTER 1
STEPPE AND FIELD

In the deep winter of 1941–2, as millions succumbed to starvation during the Siege of Leningrad, the poet Vera Inber (1890–1972) paid an extraordinary tribute to the glories of a food that was at once fundamental, and desperately short:

> I lie and think. Of what? Of bread.
> Its crust is flour-speckled, and
> the room is full of it. The furniture
> is crowded out. It is so near, and yet
> far as the promised land.
> The very best is made from fine-milled rye.
>
> The bread is bonded to my childhood.
> Domed as a hemisphere, and warm,
> fragrant with caraway. It's here,
> the span of my palm away. And, so it seems,
> if I stretched out my hand, took off my glove –
> I'd eat, and feed my husband too.

As lines formed in the small hours for pieces of so-called bread just large enough to cover an adult's palm, a real rye loaf, warm and sticky, eaten in quantity and completely on its own, was at once seductive and unattainable.

In happier times too, rye bread, the best accompaniment to vodka (in Chekhov's view), exercises a powerful pull. Sorely missed by Russians abroad, it is a buttress of tradition in the country itself. Russia remains, in the twenty-first century, the world's largest producer of rye, with 97.5 per cent of the crop going to a home market.

Yet, on a closer look, certainties dissolve. The most highly prized flour back to the medieval era was wheat. It was wheat that was used for the loaf of ritual, the karavai, which was decorated with ears of corn; it was cooked grains of wheat, flavoured with honey and dried fruit, that made kutya, the ritual dish of funerals (and in Ukraine, the Christmas Eve meal). By the late nineteenth century, richer peasant communities were starting to use wheat when they could.[1] At the other end of the scale, even rye (particularly, fine-milled forms) was out of the reach of many peasant communities. In the boggy territories of Northern Russia, barley or oaten bread was common. Flour made from birch bark was the resort of hard times. Rye, shipped to the port of Arkhangelsk, was an imported luxury, as Pyotr Chelishchev recalled in 1791. Even people of the 'middle state' sometimes resorted to potato bread, recommended by Boris Volzhin for 'times of poor harvest'.

Bread was a primal substance, its production going back centuries (the word khleb is also the word for 'grain'). This did not make its significance, or the practices associated with it, consistent. The *Domostroi* placed it at the centre of the household microeconomy. Sour bread leaven (zakvaska) was in symbiosis with brined and fermented vegetables and kvas, the small beer made from rye flour or crusts. Elena Molokhovets, though, offered few recipes for bread, and only in the case of a basic black bread recipe did she recommend a souring method. Otherwise, bought brewer's yeast was the norm. Visiting Siberia on 19 November 1862, Prince Peter Kropotkin noted in his diary that at first he had not liked the sourness of the bread there, though he'd got to like it in time.

From the early eighteenth century, city-dwellers had easy access to high-quality commercial bakeries, and were at least as familiar with the 'baton' and 'bulka' (from the French 'boule') as they were with the karavai. By 1723, Moscow (with a population of around 145,000) already had 115 professional bakers. Buying bread off the shelf eroded the sense of the sacred. While the traditional ritual of offering bread and salt to visitors (with an elaborately decorated loaf and fancy saltcellar) lived on the countryside, in cities it became the prerogative of official festivals with a 'Slavonic revival tinge' – the city governor opening a new gasworks, perhaps.

The favourite breads and baked goods of city-dwellers were those made with white flour. The ring-shaped 'kalach', the 'krendel' (a sweeter and softer version of a pretzel), the 'sitnyi', with a soft crumb and yielding crust, bagel-like 'bubliki' and tougher, long-keeping 'baranki' (the last made with their own specialist makers listed in turn-of-the-century street directories), as well as the oval 'baton' and 'bulka' – all had their own mystique. The astronomer Charles Piazzi Smyth, a close observer of Russian life when he visited in 1859, noted that the Russian countryman preferred rye, but also that a Moscow eating-house (traktir) automatically brought 'two plates of bread, too, both of them fresh and first-rate, but one of them wheaten and white, the other of rye, and therefore of a rich chocolate-brown colour'.

If baked goods made from wheat were the speciality of fancy bakers (bulochnye), rye goods came from the more down-to-earth 'pekarnya'. Rye bread was the natural pairing with salt herring. Caviar, or other refined appetisers, demanded sitnyi or bulka. As a bakery with the name 'Natural Rye Bread' in *All St Petersburg*'s 1910 edition suggested, rye was starting to be presented as the healthy choice. But the link of whiteness and refinement was tenacious – and not just when it was a choice between wheat and rye. While educated Russians took only gradually to plov, they valued polished white rice (ris).[2] Throughout the nineteenth and twentieth centuries, boiled or steamed rice was a popular accompaniment to meat dishes, or eaten as a light meal alone, and rice was used in stuffings, on its own or mixed with other ingredients. Rice pudding made with sweet milk was also a well-loved dish.

The readiness to adopt rice was probably due to its similarity to the oldest and most fundamental grain dish, kasha. Kasha, or porridge, made from all possible types of meal, was not only much older than bread but far quicker and easier to prepare. It was a staple of Russian institutions, as well as families of modest resources, as was 'kisel' or gruel, of meal and hot water.[3] Likewise, a simple 'lepyoshka', 'splodge' – anything from a thick pancake to something substantial as nan or lavash – was often the bake of choice, rather than a large loaf; failure was much less costly in terms of resources and time.[4]

Among some, the lepyoshka hardly counted as bread at all. Pushkin was disedified on his 1829 journey through the Caucasus and Turkey by 'that damned chyurek, or Armenian bread baked in the form of a lepyoshka mixed half-and-half with soot'. 'The Ostyaks never bake bread, probably because they have no ovens', Eva Felinskaya noted ten years later. But lepyoshki were common in Russian households too, from the enriched white version that was festival food in peasant households to the kinds baked with tiny amounts of suspect flour in famine times.[5]

The decline of home-baked bread continued in the Soviet period, at any rate in cities. Certainly, during the severe food crisis of 1918–19, bread, the fundamental element of rations before October 1917, was sometimes replaced by flour. The 'professorial ration' of December 1919 included 20 pounds of flour, and 7 of semolina. But much of this was no doubt turned into lepyoshki or used to make kasha and gruel, or pastry, or added to soups and sauces – or simply bartered. City-dwellers still expected to acquire bread rather than make it. If the state supply failed, they resorted to the free market, or headed for the countryside to forage. But, if supplying the population with bread was at first a problem that Bolshevik leaders struggled to solve, the aim of eradicating the private market was one to which they adhered tenaciously.

Before 1917, intervention by the state into the grain trade had been limited. In the last decades of the nineteenth century, St Petersburg's Imperial Agricultural Museum (originally founded by the Free Economic Society) became a showcase for modern agricultural machinery and plant science. Yet much of the initiative was left to private initiative and civil society, with state agencies intervening late and reluctantly even in the irrigation programme for the fertile, but drought-ridden steppe lands across the empire's southern reaches.[6] A drive to create more grain storage began only with the terrible famine of 1891–2. Otherwise, matters were left to private enterprise, which was often in the breach. Russia's first modern flour mill opened as late as 1884, in the Urals city of Ekaterinburg, while Petersburg acquired its 'mechanical steam roller mill' only two decades later, in 1907.[7] In villages, corn was usually ground in traditional stone querns; work in the fields was unmechanized. Harvesting was a community-wide effort, sometimes with hired labour also, women acting as reapers and gleaners, while the men hauled the sheaves. Any surplus was sold on a small scale.

The development of the state railway system had, on paper, the capacity to revolutionize grain deliveries, but costs and logistics meant that even in the late nineteenth century, river transport was still favoured. Whether to jetties or stations, newly harvested grain made its journey in horse-drawn waggons. The whole process benefitted an elaborate network of middlemen, beginning with the buyers at village fairs who bought grain from individual producers by the waggon-load.[8] The most notable state involvement in the grain trade related to the production of vodka, a government monopoly, which during the nineteenth century increasingly edged out beer (home-brewed 'braga' and professionally brewed 'pivo') as the alcoholic drink of choice. Restrictions on sale between 1914 and 1925, and 1985 and 1987, notwithstanding, vodka was to remain a government cash cow in the Soviet period also.

The First World War mobilized government engagement. Grain requisitions were launched, and the first municipal bakeries constructed in Moscow (1914) and Petersburg (1916). Matters did not immediately change, where practicalities rather than aspirations were concerned, after the Bolshevik Revolution. Grain production was nationalized in May 1918, and requisitioning became more purposive. However, there were under twenty state bakeries even in postrevolutionary Petrograd – a drop in the ocean.[9] Most energy was directed at getting grain into cities, against a background of civil war and economic collapse. Certainly, the Petrograd food supply committee had plans to construct two new bakeries, equipped with imported ovens. But the plans came to nothing in the meantime. A scheme to confect 'bread' from bonemeal and fish oil failed when the results, although satisfactory in nutritional terms, tasted vile.[10]

The New Economic Policy threw the population back on the free market, and escalating prices. In 1925, bread stood at between 15 and 25 kopecks a kilogram, while average wages were just 40–75 roubles a month. The plans to reform bread production were revived, and a handful of model factories, such as Bread Factory No. 1 (Moscow, 1925) and the Leningrad Tenth Anniversary of the Revolution Mechanical Bread Factory (1927), opened their doors. It was the pride of their designers that goods were untouched by human hand from start to finish. The factories themselves were pioneering exercises in rational utilitarianism, realizing in real city environments the constructivist objectives that rarely got beyond the blueprint stage. Linear, low-rise, and with large windows, they flaunted the ferro-concrete that pre-1917 flour mills, in their own way revolutionary structures, had hidden behind brick (see Figure 1.1). Along with 'factory kitchens' – whose ready-prepared, take-home meals were designed to relieve the burdens on working women – the bakeries were architectural advertisements of up-to-date food production.

A trickier problem was obtaining raw materials, as peasant growers, benefitting from free market conditions, refused to sell grain for unsatisfactory returns. From the point of view of Soviet Communism, this represented rank profiteering: the word 'kulak', now applied to class enemies in the countryside, was the slang term before 1917 for middlemen in agricultural produce. At the end of 1927, grain purchases undershot planned targets by 30 per cent, providing a stimulus and legitimation for the 1929–32 campaign of forced collectivization and grain requisition. In the long term, collectivization obliterated individual grain production in the countryside, and 'sovkhozy' (state farms), based upon the nationalized holdings of major landowners, became the engines of crop-growing. The ideal (as with industrial production) was the 'giant', highly mechanized, enterprise, in this case covering millions of hectares, serviced by machine tractor stations, and providing training for new generations of skilled workers. Whatever the propaganda value of such vast projects, the unwieldy systems of land management created difficulties that were insuperable in the long term.

During the period of the First Five-Year Plan (1928–32), there were further reforms of bread production. On 31 October 1931, a Plenary Session of the Central Community of the Communist Party passed a resolution on the mechanization of the industry and the construction of a network of modern bread factories. The first of these, Moscow's Bread Factory No. 5, adopted a radically new circular conveyor-belt system designed by Georgy Marsakov, an engineer working for the Moscow mill construction bureaucracy, who was determined that bread-making should pioneer 'the factory as machine', and that factory bread should become better than the bread made at home.

Figure 1.1 Project for a bread factory with circular conveyors by Georgy Marsakov, 1931. Lev Galpern, *The Life of Engineer Marsakov* (1934).

The original Moscow factory was followed by four more in Moscow, and two in Leningrad, all housed in landmark concrete turrets. Modernized bread production facilities were rolled out across the country in the following years. One of the first structures built in the new Soviet city of Magnitogorsk was a bread oven, functional from 1 May 1932.

Food scientists were charged with rationalizing and simplifying traditional forms of manufacture in the quest for stable, homogeneous results. The results were codified by the baking technologist Lev Auerman (employed from 1934 at the Moscow Engineering and Technological Institute of the Baking Industry). His first manual, *Wheat Bread: Raw Materials and Production*, came out in 1929. This was followed by *The Technology of Bread Baking* (1933). Auerman criticized pre-revolutionary bread production for its variability, and noted with approval that standardization had already begun in 1924–5. While observing, like Molokhovets, that, traditionally, Russian bread had been leavened using traces of the last bake's dough in the wooden kneading trough, Auerman extensively explored alternative, more modern and reliable, methods of manufacture. Substantial sections of the book addressed brewer's yeast and electric-powered kneading machines. Later editions of the book were advisory rather than investigative in stance. Sourdough leaven (zakvaska) was used for flavour, yeast leaven (zaparka) for lift; the resulting breads had a tender crumb and a crust that combined bite with give. These qualities were also codified in the official state standards for bread-baking.[11]

Just two basic types of grain were used in the Soviet baking industry: rye and wheat. Breads made of barley, millet and oats (let alone birch bark) did not make the trip from the traditional stove into the factory oven. But a degree of choice was offered. In 1938, the bread conglomerates of Leningrad Province produced dozens of different types of baked goods. In 1946, despite the straitened circumstances of the post-war years, they made, alongside 95 per cent rye and 'improved rye', six different kinds of white loaf and roll, admittedly with an admixture of unrefined flour (15 per cent). By 1951, the production of white bread was just 30 per cent less than the production of rye bread, and the range of types had expanded to include baranki and sukhariki (rusks), as well as a wider selection of loaves.

But volume remained the criterion of success. The variety of bread types on offer never came anywhere near those available before 1917, nor was this the aspiration. For the most part, there was no attempt to revive traditional names. Rather than 'sitnik' or 'kalach', late Soviet bread shops offered their customers 'baton' (a soft white cutting loaf) or 'rzhanoi' (plain rye). Names were not necessarily local: in Russian shops, you could get slightly sweet, coriander-flavoured, dark 'borodinskii' (from the great victory of 1812), but also 'darnitskii' (from the name of a district in Kyiv) and 'Riga bread', a light-brown 85 per cent rye loaf, lightly flavoured with caraway.

Personally, I only remember seeing 'Riga' loaves once; a friend had bought them in the USSR's most prestigious bread shop, the former Filippov's (known to locals by its pre-revolutionary name) at the top of Moscow's Gorky Street. She said it was Bolshoi ballerinas' favourite loaf. But even Voronezh could offer a reasonable choice: at least two sorts of rye bread and a couple of white. The last serious shortages, when even Moscow shops sold only coarse rye, came in late summer 1964. After that, grain imports solved the problem. During the 1970s and 1980s, supplies were constant. Now, bread was a comfortably familiar thing, rather than the source of fevered dreams.

The growing accessibility of bread further eroded its sacral role. Certainly, there were official attempts to revive the 'bread and salt' ritual (spurned in the early Soviet period for its association with 'Great Russian chauvinism'). A campaign launched in 1959 to create 'new traditions' suggested that instead of getting their union blessed in church, a young couple might celebrate a 'Komsomol wedding', with bread and salt to the fore. But, as writer Igor Dedkov noted in his diary on 8 June 1978, an effort by the Party bigwigs of Kostroma to greet the chairman of the Council of Ministers Aleksei Kosygin with a traditional karavai nearly hit disaster when the local bread factory repeatedly failed to bake an acceptable version of the celebrated loaf. (Eventually, a restaurant stepped in.) Ersatz folk ceremonies also provoked mirth among some who encountered them in non-official culture, such as writer Vladimir Bessonov, served bread and salt by two intelligentsia friends got up in folk costume at their dacha:

> Then the door opened, and Natalya hove in view, wearing an embroidered Ryazan-style blouse. A tight plait, as worn by unmarried girls, extended down her back, with a red silk ribbon threaded through it. She was holding a towel embroidered with various weird-looking animals, with a golden-brown karavai and a pottery salt-cellar on top. [...]
>
> 'Forgive us humble folks if things aren't right,' chirped Natalya's other half. 'So why don't you ask our dear guests in, mistress?' he added in unctuous tones.
>
> 'Come in, come in, beloved guests,' piped Natalya. 'All our wealth is for your health.'[12]

Of course, not everyone found such rituals ridiculous, or there would have been nobody to laugh at. But desacralization was a powerful trend. Bread wastage by members of the public (even in Leningrad, of all places) also pointed to changing attitudes. Soviet citizens were starting to take bread for granted.

From the point of view of quality, let alone price (pegged by subsidies), late Soviet bread was hard to beat (see Figure 1.2). It was far better than the factory-made bread produced in Britain and America. Soviet citizens were lucky that Germany, rather than the Anglophone world, had been the model. Yet bread's very consistency and availability created problems. In conditions of deficit, people did not value what they could easily get. Almost no one bothered to make bread at home. The growing numbers of home cooks attempted other types of savoury dish made from flour – pizza, for instance – rather than turning their hand to loaves.[13] Reliably available at low cost, bread made nobody's pulse quicken. I recall visiting a local store in Pechory, a small town on the Russian-Estonian border, in the early summer of 1990, a time of severe food shortages across Pskov province. Just one thing was on sale: row upon row of freshly baked, enticingly golden batony. There was not one customer in the shop.

This indifference to what was objectively a quality product helps explain the incursion into the Russian market, during the 1990s, of ready-sliced, plastic-wrapped bread. The new-style bread (often made in new facilities – the Soviet ones were now decades old) had hygiene and efficiency credentials. It was available in many varieties. Alongside Darnitsa, Borodino and plain rye (or white) loaves, you could also find baguettes, brioches, croissants and revivals of 'old Russian' types, such as khlebtsy (rye flatbreads). But whatever its novelty credentials, and date-stamped packaging, the bread widely available in supermarkets was inferior to what had been available in Soviet shops. You could get excellent bread in some independent shops aimed at an affluent market, but the cost was high even by Western standards, and the model was sourdough or 'pain au levain' rather than Soviet bread.

For all that, bread, unlike some other factory-made Soviet foodstuffs, consistently failed to figure on post-Soviet nostalgia websites and in the loud complaints of disappointed grannies. Familiarity bred contempt. What people now remembered was the delicious taste of that ham, or decorated cake, when you occasionally managed to get hold of it, and not the taste of something that you ate

Figure 1.2 Bread factory of the Southern Railway network, 1978. Belgorod Province State Archive of Recent History (GANIBO) http://ganibo.ru/belprom_4

with modest pleasure several times daily. Bread had become a victim of its own success.

The case of another dish made from dough – the pie or 'pirog' – was different, perhaps because this had been a festival rather than everyday dish since medieval times.[14] Yet stuffed bread dough was a Russian pie's most basic form. 'If rye dough is being baked, then have some of it used to make a pie, or if wheat dough is prepared, then have pies made from the flour left after sieving', the *Domostroi* suggested. Rye dough was still used in Russian villages in the nineteenth century, but among the better-off, wheat flour was standard, and it was common now to enrich the mixture.[15]

The word 'kulebyaka' (adopted into French as 'coulibiac') is usually taken by foreigners to mean 'fish pie'. But the word was used in its home country more widely: you could have a kulebyaka with meat, too (as gourmandizing numismatist Aleksei Oreshnikov noted in 1918), or indeed 'a mushroom kulebyaka' (remarked by schoolgirl Natalya Sadovnik in 1916). The defining feature of the kulebyaka was not fish as such, but sumptuous presentation. 'Pirog with fish' meant a pie of plain dough, while kulebyaka, as well as a filling that oozed with butter, also had a rich and buttery yeast crust (the sour leaven provided a sense of contrast).[16] (At the other end of the scale, in 1943, Vera Malikhieva-Mirovich resentfully remembered an aunt so mean she never served kulebyaka to poor relations, only 'wretched little plain pielets with millet in them'.)

After 1917, kulebyaka was one of the celebratory dishes that persisted in the repertoire of émigré cooks (though Merezhkovskaya recommended puff or shortcrust pastry rather than the traditional enriched yeast dough). It also had a place on the Soviet festival table. Ivan Maisky, then chairman of the Council of the League of Nations as well as the USSR's ambassador to London, boasted to his diary in May 1939 about organizing luncheon for the Council and Secretariat of the League in Geneva's Hôtel des Bergues. 'We had the traditional "Russian zakuski" – kulebyaka pie, pickled mushrooms, and other delicacies for which Soviet luncheons [...] have long been famed in Geneva.' But most pies were humbler. Factories churned them out alongside their ordinary loaves.[17] Restaurants and canteens, and more particularly buffets, had them on sale, and you could also buy them from elderly women pushing aluminium trolleys directly on the street.

The simple kinds of pies had a variety of standard fillings: mushroom, cabbage, minced meat and a purée of unsweetened dried apricot. The last were reliably delicious, the meat just as reliably the opposite (with stringy fillings and grease-soused shells). The haphazard quality acted as a spur to home cooks. A friend whose dinner repertoire normally extended to meat seared in a pan, potatoes and platefuls of sliced cucumber and tomato, would, on special occasions in the 1980s, produced her own delicious version (using flaky pastry) of Georgian cheese-filled khachapuri.

Pies used ingredients that, in big cities at least, were readily to hand, yet they had a centuries-long association with celebration food.

Even in unmodernized communal apartments in the pre-war decades, people would fire up the stove once or twice a year in order to bake a pie.

Pies large and small proved just as resilient in the post-Soviet period. One particularly successful chain, Stolle, opened its first branch (on Vasilievsky Island, St Petersburg) in 2002; twenty years later, it had over fifty branches across the country, from Kaliningrad to Krasnoyarsk, and Murmansk to Krasnodar. Elegantly presented, and with innovative fillings (chicken and broccoli, say) as well as traditional ones, Stolle pies were ensconced in the middle market. But pies were also on the repertoire of expensive restaurants; working-class districts, such as the area round the Lomonosov Porcelain Factory in St Petersburg, had their pie shops. Pies (often warm and almost always delicious) could be bought in such budget-conscious places as refectories for pilgrims to monasteries, and the canteens of libraries. And all this went on without any of the 'genuine Russian food' promotion that was aimed at, say, kvas. While the types of pie baked were not necessarily 'traditional' in every respect, the pie as a genre – whether as a portable savoury snack or as an accompaniment to soup – still laid claim to a rugged integrity.

CHAPTER 2
MEADOW AND DAIRY

'In Praise of Country Life', by Gavrila Derzhavin, written in 1798, shows a Russian country gentleman admiring his herds and flocks in the lush meadows, then sitting down to a fine roast hogget[1] 'nurtured for St Peter's Day'. He is delighted with all he sees. But the poem – a deft reworking of Horace's Second Epode – has an ironic sting in its tail. This seductive vision turns out to be the reverie of a debt purchaser, who is only 'thinking' about removal to a rural retreat.[2] The poem captures Russian (as well as Roman) ambivalence about money-making – but also the ambivalence inspired by the consumption of animal products. Abstinence from these was enjoined not only in Lent and Advent but also before lesser feasts. In Russian villages, as Derzhavin told his readers in an explanatory note, St Peter's Day (12 July) was the date for which 'the best young lambs are usually fattened, so they can be eaten to break the fast' – a seven-day one, in this case.

'Breaking the fast' sounds a Christian note amid a pagan celebration of earthly life. The foods on the gentleman's table – a smoked ham, a pot of cabbage soup (traditionally including meat), the lamb itself and not least 'various dishes made with milk' – are all 'skoromnye' (banned during fasts). Though the faithful may eat them at other times, indulgence in them has a whiff of the sinful. Virtue, it turns out, is more than simply a matter of consuming local food.

In traditional villages, cattle were the primary form of livestock, and the most resonant in symbolic terms. As 'feeder' of the family, the cow deserved awe and gratitude. A cow would never be killed and butchered for her meat, and there were special rituals for bringing her to new living quarters. Dairying was women's work, and cows were protected by a woman saint, Paraskeva, also the patron of spinning. Since the cow was an archetypal mother in her capacity to nurture, looking after a cow was an attribute of female status. In practical terms, ownership of a cow represented a major division between comfort and penury. Whether milk products were eaten at home or sent to market, they were crucial to a family's survival.

Milk production was also vital to landowners. On a country estate, where commercial shops were far distant and labour costs low, it made sense in terms of logistics as well as financially. And you could control the quality of production too. Butter, cream, sour cream and sometimes curd cheese also were regularly produced for home use, as well as milk. Those within travelling distance of a big city could also market dairy products commercially, an activity that gained in importance as estates adjusted to the hard reality of life without serfdom. By 1900, some big farms had their own city outlets. Even among better-off countryfolk, though, access to milk products was seasonal – as Dolly, Anna Karenina's sister-in-law, had to learn when on a visit to the country ('of the nine cows, some were heifers, some with their first calf, some old, and some with hard udders').

The haphazard nature of milk's availability drove a preference for cultivated dishes such as sour milk, sour cream (smetana) and curd cheese (tvorog). All were popular with peasant families, if only on festival days. In richer village households, they were eaten widely.[3] Foreign visitors noted the love of milk products in Russian society generally. James Cartmell Ridley, who visited the Urals at the end of the nineteenth century, remarked that 'many of the dishes are flavoured with cheese, while sour cream and milk enter into the composition of some of the soups, which are peculiar but palatable'. Local milk products were a pleasure of visits to rural areas: fresh cream in your tea or jugs of milk bought from the local market.

Russian villagers might hesitate to eat cows, but male calves were surplus, and would be sent to market (or occasionally butchered at home for big holidays: veal was considered a 'clean' meat). Both veal and beef were regularly part of the diet of the comfortably off. To this day, 'meat' primarily signifies the flesh of cattle. In *Evgeny Onegin*, Pushkin paid tribute to 'roast beef' served the English way, rare. The household of landowner and entrepreneur Pyotr Durnovo ate beef or veal several times a week, including most of Lent. The Russia correspondent of *The Times* Henry Sutherland Edwards remembered 'the veal of Archangel and the beef of the steppes' as delicacies of the mid-century too. By this date, some factory workers were also enjoying it, chopped up in cabbage soup, say. Annette M. B. Meakin, who visited Russia in the early twentieth century, observed that at the People's Palace in Kharkiv, run by the Society for the Promotion of Learning, there was 'a spacious and cheerful dining-room, where members can get a good dinner for a merely nominal price. Five kopecks (one penny farthing) are charged for a large plate of vegetable soup, and the same sum for a substantial plate of meat or pudding'. The widespread view that only a diet with plenty of meat was healthy both reflected and enhanced consumption.

If dairying was ensconced in the Russian heartlands, particularly the areas round big cities and the north and west, the appetite for meat was primarily fed by Russia's neighbours to the south and east, from the farmers of the Ukrainian steppes to the nomad herders of Central Asia. In 1886, the Russian journalist Anatoly Bakhtiarov put the numbers of cattle arriving for slaughter in St Petersburg at 1000 per day, or over a quarter million a year. By the 1910s, numbers had more than doubled.[4] This was only the start: calves were often butchered in smaller abattoirs attached to meat shops. Customers who could not afford the more prestigious cuts, such as fillet or rump, could purchase neck, skirt or indeed oxtail, breast or feet. One of Russia's most popular meat dishes, 'studen', is a brawn-like composition of pulled beef or veal in jelly that takes rich advantage of the gelatinous, meltingly tender character of these cheaper cuts.[5] Delicacies such as smoked ox tongues aside, the refined preferred not to touch animal innards. But for those short of funds, visiting a vendor of offal such as liver, spleen, hearts and lights (lungs), was the most accessible way to get meat.[6] Whichever way, meat prices were highly sensitive, even triggering discussions in the Petersburg City Duma.

A move to the big city meant not only eating more of what you were used to but switching to unaccustomed foods. By traditional belief, pigs were unclean animals.[7] One looks in vain for the rich involvement with the animal that Claudine Fabre-Vassas has traced in French culture.[8] But Ukrainians relished pork fat (salo), as did Russians in south-west border areas. Russians in the social elite seem to have eaten at least some pork back to medieval times. As Derzhavin's 'In Praise of Village Life' suggests, by the late eighteenth century, they were also familiar with cured pork products, such as hams. A century later, such products had an established place on the table even for religious holidays (Molokhovets suggested a smoked boar's head for Easter). Certainly, as late as the 1880s, the 40,000 pigs going for slaughter in Russia's most Westernized city, St Petersburg stood at less than a third of the number of cattle. Yet this represented a rise of about 50 per cent compared with the start of the decade. In the First World War, prices for pork rose higher than for any other meat.

As for sheep, the prime areas were in mountainous parts of the Empire, where fat-tailed types, such as the hardy Karachaev breed, were preferred. But sheep were also kept in some Russian villages. Wealthier peasants in Kaluga province might have a dozen or so, and even poorer families a couple.[9] However, most mutton and lamb was eaten locally, since transport costs were high relative to marketable weight. It was only in winter, when the animals could be killed close to where they lived, and despatched in frozen form, that the trade reached any dimensions in Petersburg and Moscow.

The growing appetite for meat in cities had a direct impact on producers. The situation was particularly advantageous to large farmers. Between 1876 and 1900, while the herds belonging to landowners and leaseholders in Stavropol Province increased by a factor of ten, those of peasant communities slightly declined. But by the late nineteenth and early twentieth centuries, peasant farmers were also sending meat to market in ever larger amounts. Agricultural censuses of the 1880s to the 1910s recorded rising surpluses, province-wide, of beef in Orenburg, Astrakhan, Ufa and Samara provinces, and the Ukrainian Black Sea; veal and pork in Tver, Pskov and Novgorod provinces; and poultry in Moscow, Vladimir, Kaluga, Yaroslavl and St Petersburg provinces.

As the demand for milk and meat grew, so the issue of how to satisfy it became more pressing. Already in the eighteenth century, Russian landowners had become interested in breed improvement, which at the time usually meant the importation of foreign animals to ennoble local ones. This enthusiasm continued into the nineteenth century: among the favoured breeds were Simmenthal, Ayrshire, Tirolean, Ällgau and English Shorthorn, as kept by famous gentleman breeder Vasily Pashkov on his estates in Tambov. The Ministry of State Property endorsed these enthusiasms, showcasing high milk- and meat-yield cattle at exhibitions, in the displays of St Petersburg's Agricultural Museum, and in its publications. Active also in the cause of agricultural improvement were the zemstva, or local authorities, set up in 1864, and voluntary organizations such as the Imperial Moscow Agricultural Society and Free Economic Society. Thanks to their efforts, and to those of educational institutions such as the Petrovsky Academy in Moscow, farmers could now rely on qualified advice about animal keeping, rather than the compilations of snippets that circulated during the late eighteenth and early nineteenth centuries.

One area of close interest was cheese-making. From at least the early nineteenth century, Russian gourmets had developed a taste for, say, the 'runny Limburger' mentioned in Pushkin's *Evgeny Onegin*.[10] By mid-century, cheese was also produced on a small scale in Russia itself. Radetsky's *Almanac for Gastronomes* approvingly mentioned in particular Meshchersky cheese, made by one of Russia's premier aristocratic families on their 10,000-hectare estate in Tver province, and selling for about the same price as the Swiss cheese that it imitated. Popularizing cheese production in less rarefied circles was the mission of Nikolai Vereshchagin, who had studied artisanal cheese-making in Switzerland.[11] His Tver province village cheesery, opened in 1867, launched a movement to set up cooperatives (artels) in rural areas and to involve peasant producers. By 1869, there were already functioning cheeseries in Novgorod, Smolensk, Yaroslavl and Rybinsk provinces as well as Tver.[12] In the late 1890s, there were villages in Yaroslavl where villagers drank skimmed milk themselves because whole milk was reserved for cheese-making.[13] When it came to eating, cheese was very much an optional extra for an affluent public – a popular zakuska, whether served before a meal or at an informal, improvised feast.

A more significant development in overall social terms was the rise of pig keeping, previously marginal among landowners as well as peasants. Before the late nineteenth century, activity went little further than the raising of sucking pigs (fattened up on skimmed milk from the dairy) for the profitable Easter market. The first comprehensive manual, by Ottomar Rohde (translated from the German), appeared only in 1875. An appendix about Russian pig-keeping written by the translator for the second edition suggested that overall numbers in 1876 had increased only 4 per cent over twenty-five years, and that activity at grassroots level was concentrated in south-western areas of the Empire (Ukraine, Belarus). Pyotr Kuleshov's *Pig-Keeping*, originally published in 1888, gave comparable information for the end of the following decade. Yet the fact that both books were reprinted several times bespoke their popularity.

While Kuleshov mainly emphasized the export potential of pork and pork products, he also pointed to an emerging market in Russian cities. Russian hams might be of inferior quality, so far as a fussy city market was concerned, but the 'population of the poor and factory workers' was glad enough to buy the forequarters that the delicatessen market left untouched. By the late 1890s, as Tenishev Bureau informants reported, pigs were widely kept in villages.[14] In the wealthier places, there would be more than one pig: two or three pigs being fed up for Christmas, say, alongside four dairy cows. Less affluent families might have a single pig. Now, even poorer peasants in some areas of central Russia sometimes put meat in soups.[15]

In the early twentieth century, advice aimed at peasant pig-keepers started to appear, tirelessly reminding readers that pigs could live on scraps, matured quickly and fetched high prices at market. But not just any pig would do: 'The unimproved Russian pig produces fibrous meat that tastes no good', warned a poster produced by the Imperial Agricultural Museum in the early 1910s. More realistically, a 1912 booklet on intensive pig-rearing, published in the 'Village Library' series, extolled the virtues of imported English pigs, particularly the Yorkshire or White pigs and Berkshires, but also assured its readers that native breeds were hardy, were economical feeders and produced excellent meat.

In reality, livestock improvement was definitely for the moneyed classes: premium cattle were exchanged on networks running from Prussian barons to Russian empresses, then down to princes, countesses and retired colonels out in the wilds of Tver, who fed and housed their animals at least as well as they did their servants (see Figure 2.1). Villagers preferred to stick with their hardy local breeds, who were happy to scrabble for food in the forest or under the snow. Indeed, by the end of the nineteenth century, some members of the educated population shared the preference for native beasts, rather than 'pampered' animals 'who hang round the house all the time, as though expecting alms'.

For their part, the Bolsheviks took stock rearing in hand from the beginning. A decree of 13 July 1918 nationalized all pedigree animals, initiated an inventory by veterinary commissions under the Land Management Committee, prohibited requisitioning by the army and put the animals at the disposal of local soviets, communes, organizations and individual farmers. A government-sponsored research centre, 'Breed Culture', was created to spearhead work on

Figure 2.1 Strelka, a prize-winning cow of the 'native' Kholmogory breed from the royal farm at Tsarskoe Selo. *Report of the First All-Russian Cattle Exhibition*, 1869.

selection, which also took place at the Moscow Institute of Agricultural Science's Experimental Station (led by Mikhail Ivanov), and in the regions.

Admiration for foreign breeds remained widespread. 'The [English] shorthorn', wrote a professor of agronomy in 1925, 'is very widely dispersed in cultured nations'. Such 'civilized' breeds, in the eyes of the day, were models for the 'backward' USSR.

A central aim from the start was the provision of milk in adequate amounts. As Lenin put it, 'every child from a poor family must get a good-quality bottle a day'. Larger milk plants were nationalized in 1918–19, though distribution through the cooperative movement and indeed private vendors continued. From 1925, a drive began to create hygienic processing facilities, usually sited in rural areas near large cities, so that milk could be screened for TB and other zoonotic diseases.

Providing high-quality milk also meant distribution of processed forms. Systematic research into sour milk production began not long after the October Revolution. Microbiologist Lyubov Gorovits-Vlasova discovered in 1923 that it was possible to create an effective probiotic starter for soured mare's milk (kumiss), widely produced by traditional means in Central Asia, and popular as a health cure. Samples of the finished product were dried, and then added to fresh milk. While this did not lead to the appearance in shops and cafés across Russia of kumiss, a similar process with cow's milk produced the sour and slightly fizzy kefir, for sale in Soviet cities from the 1920s.[16] Promoted as a 'dietary milk product', it was so common by the late 1930s that fussy buyers complained about getting it rather than sour cream.[17] Sour cream, rather than fresh cream, was likewise the preferred product of Soviet factories. 'Dietary milk products' were widely available in shops and public catering in the following decades too, and continued to figure in advisory literature.

Curd cheese (*tvorog*) likewise remained a staple. It was available in factory-processed form, but you could also buy it at private markets, and later, collective farm markets. More elusive was actual cheese. Already a luxury food, it rose steeply in price during the First World War. By 1916, Dutch-style cheese cost more than five times as much as it had in 1914 (while butter and eggs had merely doubled). 'I ate too much Dutch cheese at Suvchinsky's yesterday – it's such a delicacy', Alexandre Benois confessed on 26 November 1917. 'Milk, milk products, and cheese – there are tiny quantities available, of poor quality, and so expensive they're quite out of most people's reach', complained historian Stepan Veselovsky (27 January 1920).

Occasionally, cheese was available through state distribution (for instance, Nikolai Tagantsev recorded on 20 July 1921 that you could get Meshchersky cheese with your ration card, and pay a bit less than for butter). But this seems to have been privately produced. Marietta Shaginyan, visiting Armenia in the summer of 1926, saw 'a cheese factory looking just like a sanatorium'. She heard that a local politician had set up a whole chain to churn out the perennial favourite, Swiss-style cheese. In Russia itself, supplies were still short and lines long.[18] After the end of NEP, ordinary stores simply ran out. 'There was nothing at all in the shop but cardboard models of cheese', lamented writer Mikhail Prishvin, on 24 February 1930. To get the real thing, Muscovites had to surrender their valuables in Torgsin.[19]

Cheese, though, was one of the delicacies restored to favour under the Second Five-Year Plan. A landmark was the construction in Moscow of Russia's first factory for processed cheese, opened in 1934. Its output was at first small, and complaints about shortages continued in diaries. But in the early 1940s, food technicians at the plant evolved a new method of manufacture by which cheese deemed unfit for sale because of low fat content was enriched with butterfat. Processed cheese was to become a ubiquitous product in the late Soviet USSR, available, because of its long shelf life, when other foods had sold out. At the same time, the most popular types, such as 'Viola' (imported from Finland from 1956) and 'Amber' (its Soviet imitator), were subject to shortage. Thus, William Pokhlyobkin could recommend 'Amber' in his *Entertaining Cookery* (1983) – for use, say, in 'soupe a l'oignon' – and not disillusion his readers.

The most ideologically significant animal product throughout Soviet history, however, was meat. Soviet administrators subscribed to the early twentieth-century educated consensus that meat was a vital food, exercising an 'excitatory' effect on the organism that vegetables lacked. Meat was included in ration allocations, and there were efforts to place meat outlets under the control of the state and cooperatives. Even if the meat actually on sale was second-rate, getting it there was vital.[20]

State control, however, was dislocated during collectivization, when peasant communities slaughtered and ate their animals rather than hand them over, provoking catastrophic shortages. One attempt to rectify the situation was the promotion of intensive pig-rearing. Pyotr Stroev's painting of a contented sow with her litter, *In the Pig-Rearing State Farm* (1932), provided an evocative image. Collective as well as state farms were encouraged to take up pig-breeding, as were individual peasants on their private plots. By 1940, 36 per cent of state farms had piggeries, and from 1930 to 1935, the USSR had as many pigs as beef cattle and veal calves put together. Cattle competed with the human population for scarce grain reserves. The pig's capacity to live on scraps was a godsend.

Alongside the transformation of animal rearing went a transformation of meat processing. In the late 1880s, the St Petersburg central abattoir was still manned by traditional butchers in leather aprons, who despatched animals with sharpened daggers. Though laboratory screening was customary, a significant proportion of meat with parasitic infestations, Bakhtiarov noted, made its way into smoking and sausage-making because butchers were reluctant to throw it away. Adequate refrigeration was often lacking. Many smaller butchers had primitive killing facilities in a back room, and here inspection of the results was in abeyance. As *The Marketing of Food Products* lamented in 1928, 'Russian meat is an extremely variable foodstuff'.

The 1933 edition of the same book omitted this comment. Instead, it hymned the surge of meat production in state and collective farms, treasure-houses of 'cultured breeds'. Meat processing was not mentioned, partly because it was still a work in progress. A decree of 29 September 1931, 'On the Development of the Meat and Preserved Meat Industry', anticipated the creation of fifty-seven new plants, including eight 'giants' ('in the most important worker centres, Moscow, Leningrad, and Sverdlovsk', as well as six key meat-producing regions). But it was the Second Five-Year Plan, launched in 1933, when the plants began opening.

'Giant' plants were indeed massive facilities, their entrances graced with pillars and statues of cattle. Yet, as an album on the Leningrad Meat Plant, *A Giant of the Meat Industry*, emphasized, they were totally up to date in terms of mechanization and efficiency. Everything, from slaughter to packing, was housed on one site. There were special facilities for housing animals after the journey, so that they could rest and regain weight lost in travel. Waste disposal was handled carefully. Animal welfare had a place: for instance, an electrical stunner was used before the animal was killed and blood drained (see Figure 2.2).

Pork had a crucial role in the new meat plants' planned output. According to the 29 September 1931 decree, the eight 'giants' were

Figure 2.2 Photomontage, 'Slaughter and Meat Processing', *A Giant of the Meat Industry*, 1936.

supposed to process 5.4 million pigs per year, double the combined numbers of sheep and cows (1.3 million and 1.4 million). Much of this ended up as cured pork. An earlier decree (15 July 1931) required every meat-processing plant to have a sausage workshop.

The 1933 edition of *The Marketing of Food Products* dropped the elaborate tables showing individual cuts of fresh meat that had appeared in the 1928 edition, but included copious new material on salting, drying, smoking and canning. Sausage took pride of place. In pre-revolutionary days, the book informed readers, 'it was impossible to make sufficient and appropriate use of the so-called secondary products of meat processing and leftovers from the division of the carcase, such as head meat, intestines, stomach, and so on'. Now things were different: 'The equipment of sausage factories with the latest technology has made it possible to transform both meat as such, and the above by-products, into first-class sausage.' The recommended process involved hand-trimming and chopping of the sausage's whole meat constituents – but also use of mechanical mincing or emulsification of the rest. Sausage, particularly of 'the second class', became a tactful way of using up the innards of the beast. Now discreetly known as 'subproducts', these were no more popular with socially advantaged Russians than they had been before 1917. 'The so-called goulash turned out to be made of lights [lungs], (a horse's?) with potato, in a very spicy sauce. I couldn't eat it', complained Mikhail Prishvin on 11 July 1930.

During the Second World War, livestock numbers suffered badly. There were nearly 20 per cent fewer beef cattle in 1945 than in 1940, and the pig population stood at less than half its pre-war numbers, the lowest for more than thirty years. Not surprisingly, increasing meat production was a key theme of the Fifth Five-Year Plan, announced in 1946. As well as taking fresh meat production back to pre-war levels, the Plan aimed to boost the production of preserved meat and pre-prepared meat dishes. Meat was listed in the individual production targets for the different republics, as well as the schedule of overall objectives.

The ambitious targets for greater meat availability again put pork centre stage. In 1953, pigs once more overtook numbers of cattle reared for meat, a position they retained throughout the Soviet period (and indeed into the 2000s). But there was also a search for other meat-bearing animals that could be raised more economically than cows. Lamb and mutton, the preferred meats in much of the Caucasus and Central Asia, remained a minority taste among Russians. Indeed, across the USSR generally, sheep raised for meat, as opposed to tallow and wool, represented just 8 per cent of the population even at the start of the 1970s. Despite a 20 April 1972 decree of the Council of Ministers ordering the creation of large-scale, mechanized sheep farms for the production of wool and meat, the market share of lamb and mutton reached only 10 per cent in 1980, and in 1985, slumped to 6 per cent.

There was far more success with mass-producing chicken, a meat whose taste was, from the Russian point of view, pleasantly bland, rather than disagreeably pronounced. As in other countries before the introduction of intensive farming, chicken had traditionally been a delicacy. In peasant households, eggs were a rare treat, and killing their provider would have been prodigal. A cockerel not sent to market was a dish for a big festival.[21] Even in relatively privileged circles, chicken pie (kurnik) was a party dish. According to Odoevsky's Dr Puf, a chicken cost the same as a brace of hazel hen or a quarter of the cost of an entire side of veal. Nothing on the bird was wasted: an elegant soup might be made of chicken broth and morels, or the giblets used for a heartier one.

After 1917, too, a chicken remained a once-in-a-year event for many. As with other types of farm animal, the emphasis at first was on breed improvement, rather than acceleration of production, though hen batteries began to be organized on a small scale in the 1930s.[22] The main interface between the state and the farming population was the small-scale workshop for processing poultry, where butchery was done entirely by hand – a sign of the numbers to be accommodated.[23]

Poultry farming did not increase substantially in scale until well after the war. The watershed was a decree of the Central Committee and Council of Ministers, passed on 3 September 1964, introducing industrial poultry production as a nationwide objective. Between 1965 and 1970, egg production swelled by more than 50 per cent, while government purchases of poultry meat from collective farms almost tripled. A discussion at the Leningrad Regional Committee of the Communist Party in 1979 gives a sense of the scale of the changes: meat production would rise over two years from 184,000 to 260,000 tonnes, 'and the hen batteries will produce close to two billion eggs per year'.[24]

Meat remained short during the Soviet Union's last years also, in part because availability fed demand. But production was to a high extent standardized. Most cattle were local variants of crossbred Friesians, a handy dual-purpose type also popular in America and Western Europe. An overwhelming proportion of pigs had English Large White as well as local blood in their veins. Products were equally unvarying: tinned stew, 'The Tourist's Breakfast' – a kind of Soviet equivalent of Spam – and various types of minced sausage, usually pork ('The Doctor's Choice' offered digestible chicken). Where fresh meat was concerned, sophisticated butchery was in abeyance. 'A kilo of meat' might mean anything from bones to a relatively choice cut (or shreds of one). Frugal cooks, and institutional catering, made heavy reliance on different forms of meat ball, which differed mainly in terms of shape and the amount of bread added.[25] Ambitious cooks 'made friends with a butcher' (a euphemism for various types of favour exchange). Or they could benefit from the overall disdain for 'subproducts' and discover that traditionally prized examples of these, such as tongue, were easy to buy.[26]

Meat was the heart of the meal. If pushed, one could open a tin ('The Tourist's Breakfast' mashed into fried potatoes was a popular meal among the students from factory-worker backgrounds in our Voronezh hostel). Russian students living in Estonia, on the other hand, would regularly buy blood pudding – the cheapest available sausage. If you (or your grandparents) came from a village background in southern Russia, there would be home-prepared pork back fat (salo), devoured with fresh garlic scapes.[27] The better-off might choose a 'ready to cook' option, such as trimmed escalopes, from a 'culinary shop' (offering quality at a premium). Despite the efforts at standardization, meat remained 'an extremely variable foodstuff' in the 1970s and 1980s, just as it had in the 1920s. Assuming that you could get it in the first place.

One effect of the long-term attention to meat provision above all was that Russia, formerly noted for rather low meat consumption, became one of the most 'carnivorous' countries in the world. At the same time, people often grumbled about the quality of the meat available. 'I like *Western* sausage', said a friend in 1980: 'Here they put all kinds of junk in it.' To anyone who also used ordinary shops, the most startling section of the hard-currency-only food store near the Kiev Station in Moscow was the one with cured meats: made in top Soviet factories, they had no resemblance at all to what was usually available. And in the denunciatory documentary, *We Can't Live Like This* (1990), it was a display of German sausage that Director Sergei Govorukhin chose as background for a dramatic rant: So why don't we have all this too?

Standardization worked better in the case of milk products. But here, too, there were issues of supply. Fresh milk could disappear for days or even weeks, and when on sale, regularly vanished early in the morning. Powdered milk was supposed to act as a standby, but despite enhanced production in the 1970s, that too often ran short. While the mechanization programme carried out in the late 1950s simplified processing, enhanced volume and speed brought problems of their own – as with a mass outbreak of dysentery that gripped a small town in Leningrad Province for four months in late 1956 and early 1957, and was rapidly traced to the local milk factory. Nearly 800 kilos of suspect smetana was identified. Rather than being destroyed, this was used for clarified butter production.[28]

Like intensive agriculture, industrial food production was both the victim and the cause of environmental harm. Radiation contamination in hen batteries bespoke the former, mass poultry deaths from *Pseudopestis avium* the latter.[29] Conditions were awful for workers too. In 1975, employees of milk factories and dairy farms across Leningrad province raised complaints about living conditions (homes with no drains or gas), poor pay and holiday rights, inhuman working hours, substandard medical support, the non-availability of common rooms, or even basins and toilets, in the workplace and the dearth of fish, sausage or even meat in local shops – though vodka flowed in abundance.[30] Those who cared for animals, or despatched them in abattoirs, and worked in such conditions, did not always have much charity to spare for their charges.[31] Even if they did, the practicalities might defeat them, as in the case of an idealistic young vet who had piglets die on her hands because there was no feed.[32]

The increasing problems of Soviet meat and milk production in the last decades of the country's existence were reflected also in the steep rise of imports. While never on the same scale as shipments of grain, imports of meat doubled between 1975 and 1985, and by 1990, it was the third largest imported foodstuff. Imports of milk products ran at lower levels, but never fell below 150,000 tonnes per year after 1978.

Dependence on imported milk and meat was a feature of the post-Soviet period also. But structural investment by the state and private business made an appreciable dent on imports after 2000. The counter-sanctions campaign against EU countries after 2014 accelerated this process, with a surge in home-produced pork – even if the favourite Russian pig was actually a foreign one, the Large White (customers now preferred a leaner animal than the traditional crossbreeds).

Whichever way, the animal products that reached Russian shoppers (with the exception of artisanal cheese from home or abroad, a microscopic niche in the market) were produced by large-scale operations. This applied as much to the delicious smetana sold out of enamel bowls at markets, and made in the dairies of privatized collective and state farms, as to the branded yoghourts on the supermarket shelf. A farm keeping Jerseys in the 2020s UK might run to 150 cows; its Voronezh equivalent had over 1000. There were exceptions – Altai lamb, goat's curd – but the eggs you could buy, however nicely packaged, still came from batteries, and even farmer's market chicken tended to taste of fishmeal. In a revival of the situation back in the 1860s, some top restaurants started their own farms, but – as of the early 2020s, anyway – organic production had still to make real impact on mainstream eating, whether at home or beyond.

CHAPTER 3
POND AND RIVER

In 1826, Alexander Pushkin sent his friend, the cynic and wit Sergei Sobolevsky, advice in rhyme on how to survive a long and tedious journey from Moscow to Novgorod. Take good wine along – you'll find none on the journey. Snack on parmesan with macaroni in Tver, and Pozharsky cutlets in Torzhok. But save room for Yazhelbitsy (a substantial village on the main Moscow-St Petersburg road), because the biggest feast awaits you there:

> They'll bring trout for your inspection!
> Have them boiled immediately.
> When they're blue in all directions,
> Pour in the soup some good Chablis.
>
> So the dish makes you quite happy
> You can add, when piping hot,
> To your soup some ground black pepper,
> And some onion, finely chopped.

After such resplendent nosh, it would have been almost a relief to find no fresh 'Valdai herrings' (a fish from the local lake) at the next stop.

Pushkin's recommendation for the pescatarian highpoint of the day was untraditional in one respect. The customary addition to fish soup, (ukha), was a gout of vodka rather than Chablis (the idea was to remove the muddy taste that can be a hazard of river fish). Everything else – the careful inspection of the fish (preferably alive) before it was poached with minimum seasonings, and served in the resulting liquor – followed custom to the letter. Certainly, those who wished could cook the fish in pre-prepared fish bouillon ('double ukha'), and perhaps even poach lesser fish in the bouillon before adding the star of the show ('triple ukha'). But with such a delicacy as trout served blue, elaboration was unnecessary.

Exactly these characteristics – freshness, simplicity and speed – were regularly remarked by Westerners enjoying Russian fish cuisine in the nineteenth century.[1] St Petersburg, unlike Vyzhelbitsy or Valdai, was short of local fish, apart from its early summer glut of cucumber-scented smelt (koryushka). But you could get a wide variety of brought-in live fish from holding pens (sadki) directly in the water of the local rivers. As late as the early twentieth century, according to street directories, there was even one by Anichkov Bridge in the middle of Nevsky Prospect.

If the capital could offer gourmets imported delicacies, local fish cookery was the pride of the regions. River fish were treasured above all. On the Volga, in the category of 'red' (i.e. 'fine') fish came sturgeon, salmon and 'belorybitsa' (a member of the Salmonidae family, known in Alaska as sheefish), while everything else was classed as 'common' (see Figure 3.1). Other rivers had similar classifications. All the same, many 'lesser' fish had culinary status also: carp, pike, Caspian roach (vobla, traditionally dried as a chewy accompaniment to drinks), freshwater bream, pike-perch and an impressive range of different types of whitefish (sig, cf. the Finnish *sikka*).

Figure 3.1 Salmon. *The Marketing of Food* (1933).

Many towns on major rivers were centres of commercial fishing (Rybinsk on the Volga, for instance). But fish could be a pleasure of summers in small country places, too. Painter Vasily Vereshchagin, staying near Rostov Velikii in the 1890s, enjoyed Ishnya eel-pouts ('not at all dear'), and large crawfish, which were even cheaper. Volzhin's *Encyclopaedia* (1842) included a resplendent array of fish pies, cold fish in jelly, fish spit-roasted, fried, poached and steamed. In some dishes, plain butter or smetana (or both) set off the delicate flavour of whitefish or river bream, while carp and other types of fish with more pronounced flavour were treated to blasts of dried fruit and spices.

But if river fish were ingrained in Russian tradition (the Volga has archaeological evidence of fishing back to Neolithic times), sea fish were indispensable too. A St John's Day menu at Solovki monastery included both cod with kvas and herring with vinegar, and monastery fish soup.[2] Gourmets might enthuse over imported lobster and prawns, but herring, usually invoked in the diminutive, 'selyodka', was the people's fish. 'A herring is plenty for ten, but a chicken will hardly feed two', ran one ironic saying. Vobla was popular for snacks (as Stephen Graham remembered, 'fish-ends' clung to the floor of every third-class railway carriage). Selyodka had the substance of an actual meal. People enjoyed fresh herring fried, but it was commoner packed into barrels and salted, a stalwart of meatless eating in starters and in main dishes – stuffed, dressed with sauce or turned into fish balls.

The abundance of Russian waters meant there was little use for fishponds.[3] Exceptional was Vladimir Vrassky's experimental breeding station at Nikolskoe, Novgorod province, founded in 1860, where he developed a successful technique for inseminating fish eggs (the so-called 'dry method'). Remarkable as it was, Vrassky's initiative also remained an isolated effort; indeed, it was the national centre into the late Soviet period also. Rather than being hatched, fish was caught in open waters. The bard of the sporting pursuit of fish was Sergei Aksakov, whose 1858 essay 'Some Words on Angling in the Early Spring and Late Autumn' evoked mist rising over the river as small birds darted and the fisherman immersed himself in pursuit of the quarry. But suburban parks were as likely a destination as country estates.

For amateur anglers, like hunters and gatherers, the catch was less important than the taking part; the best sporting fish didn't necessarily make the best eating. However, Aksakov's *Notes on Angling* (1847) provided some culinary hints of a simple kind alongside the advice on fishing tackle, bait and the technique of casting. Ruffe was delicious in jelly; roach didn't make good fish soup, but could be potted in sour cream; pike cooked straight from the river was an excellent dish.

In peasant Russian society, fishing was more for subsistence than sport, though the borders could be porous. Stephen Graham recalled meeting at the start of the 1910s 'picturesque tramp fishermen in ragged clothes and fearfully leaky boots'. They shared 'the best of fish dinners – pike, perch, or bream fried with butter in my tramping saucepan'. In the evening he would meet 'the huntsman going home with a string of fat duck and dainty sandpipers on his back, the dog at his heel', while 'the fisherman would be returning from the market with bread and vodka'. Such solitaries, devoted to the chase, but also living off it, were transitional figures between pure amateurs and the country-dwellers who lived by fishing. Here, the chosen tackle was nets rather than rods (unless for very small fish), and the catch was brought in by groups working together. In April 1856, the playwright Aleksandr Ostrovsky watched villagers in Tver Province use dug-out canoes and baskets woven from willow twigs, which they strung across the river between fans of pine and fir needles. The Russian Ethnographical Museum in St Petersburg has photographs of similar work carried out by women.

By no means all fishing was done in this primal manner. By the end of the eighteenth century, fish was enough of a business among Russians in the north-west that they could afford to buy fishing rights out of Reval (now Tallinn) which were beyond the pocket of locals. At the start of the 1840s, Ekaterina Avdeeva encountered fishermen on Chudo (Peipsi) Lake (on the borders of Russia and modern Estonia) who during the short fishing season were able to earn 1000 roubles per net, a substantial sum at the time. Academician Karl Ernst von Baer already expressed anxieties in 1853 about over-fishing on a commercial basis, and catches in the Volga-Caspian area, the premium place for 'fine' river fish, bore him out. They rose steeply in the second half of the nineteenth century, but catches of several species, notably belorybitsa and river bream, were down to their 1857 levels by 1910. Astrakhan's invaluable sturgeon trade was increasingly reliant on the marine catch.

The monetary value of the catch meant fishing generated far more interest from the state than the harvesting of other natural resources. Regulation of rights went back to 1649, and tax to 1704. But the state's intervention was not just financial. Peter I's decree on revenue also created the Astrakhan Fishing Office, responsible for quality control and regulation of fishing practices. Tighter measures came in 1862: a ban on fishing in estuary waters, control of net use and the imposition of a close season. The Fishing Industry Expedition (set up in 1803 as a successor to the Astrakhan Fishing Office) organized expert surveys on fish stocks, and from 1857, the state also sponsored experimental work in fish farming. But involvement was limited, not extending, for instance, to investment in the technology of fishing, which was still heavily reliant on traditional nets and harpoons. Outside the winter months, when caught, fish froze naturally, the sole widespread commercial forms of preservation were drying and salting; the first commercial canning plant opened only in 1911.

The situation was the more remarkable given heavy demand for fish. During Russia's many Orthodox fasts, fish-eating came into its own. The sole permitted animal product, it was the most luxurious food of abstinence. Enriched pies, or elaborate braises, could be made with oil instead of butter. More modest delicacies included fish with fermented beetroot, and 'Trans-Volga pies' of sourdough filled with salmon or chopped sturgeon fins. You could cook eel in red wine or enjoy champagne with your caviar. Fish eating did not smack of desperation.

In the early Soviet period, the retreat of religion to the margins of life, and the exaltation of meat as the primary source of protein, brought about a decline in the status of fish. Direct state management began in 1919, but in the first years, the main effort went into setting up research institutes. The dilapidated infrastructure received little attention. River and lake fishing remained artisanal. Ocean catches were mainly made up of mackerel, anchovy and the inevitable herring. Selyodka, as regularly provided on state rations, and the vobla chewed by convicts in cattle-trucks, had a dismal resonance. Even prestigious types of fish suffered by association. Complaining about food shortages on 22 October 1930, engineer Ivan Popov bewailed 'the pikeperch nightmare: six months with nothing but fish'. It didn't help that the deliveries weren't always in prime condition; to quote a famous joke in Mikhail Bulgakov's *Master and Margarita*: 'They've sent sturgeon of the second freshness'. On 12 September 1932, the People's Commissariat of Food Supply introduced compulsory weekly 'Fish Days' in all public catering outlets, but the measure lasted only a year.

State intervention into fishing during the 1930s went along two different paths: the 'stick' of state control and the 'carrot' of investment. On 7 April 1934, a decree of the People's Commissariat of Supply instituted the Fisheries and Waterways Board (Glavrybvod) as a general industry inspectorate. Fishermen were forced to join collectives (a process 86 per cent complete by 1935). But on the side of encouragement, there were at least limited efforts to explore new types of catch (for instance, sprats and grey mullet in the Black Sea). Along with the promotion of conserves generally, fish began to be more widely canned: mackerel or sprats, say, in oil, pickled, in its own juice, and in tomato sauce. All the same, levels of fish consumption remained very low – under six kilos a year per head, according to figures from 1937.

Development of the fisheries became more purposive after the war, under an enterprising minister, People's Commissar of the Fish Industry Aleksandr Ishkov, who remained in charge for most of the next forty years. While river and lake fishing had a negligible role compared with its pre-1917 importance, ocean fishing was energetically developed. From the late 1940s, Soviet deep-water trawlers pushed far offshore. Pride of place was given to Kamchatka crab, whose gigantic proportions echoed the era's emphasis on size. The tender white meat, less fibrous than the common crab's, required little picking over, and suited the canning process. Much of it went for export, but some was marketed for home consumption, still labelled in wonky English, 'Packed by floating canneries of fish industry of USSR'.[4]

At the end of the next decade, the Soviet Union started to acquire huge floating fish factories built in Poland, beginning with the Severodvinsk, launched in 1958.[5] Fish consumption rose between 1950 and 1960 by nearly 50 per cent. But disdain persisted. 'For some reason, there was no meat, so I had to get two portions of potato dumplings [*varenyky*], a bottle of kefir, and some cold cod', Nikolai Kozakov, visiting Kharkiv, complained on 25 July 1962. Even in 1960, average annual consumption was just 9 kg per year, barely half of what Soviet nutritionists considered the desirable minimum (16 kg). In 1963, fish was the lowest of all categories of food in terms of average monthly spend, irrespective of income group: four times less than expenditure on meat, and more than twenty times less than expenditure on milk.[6] Tinned fish in tomato sauce was quite popular in the Stalin era, but under Khrushchev its appeal slumped.[7]

Over the next twenty years, as meat shortages became more acute, the promotion of fish-eating intensified. A Central Committee and Council of Ministers decree of 26 October 1966 set out plans. The fish catch should be boosted, including freshwater fish inside the USSR; transport infrastructure should be improved, particularly the supply of refrigerated railway wagons; a chain of fish-processing plants should be set up; and more specialist facilities in shops should be created. Factory ships travelled long distances north for cold-water species, but by the 1970s, they were also voyaging as far afield in the other direction as Mozambique.

Compared with deep-sea fishing, freshwater fishing (contrary to national tradition) was a small-scale activity. One issue was the extent of pollution to the waterways that had gone in step with crash industrialization. In Siberia, oil and chemical spills had devastating ecological effects. Baikal, famed for its whitefish species such as omul and Arctic grayling, represented the exception rather than the rule. Contamination of waterways may have been a factor inhibiting fish farming also. Certainly, it was not until 1978 that legislation to develop this on a large scale was set in place, and even then, the effects seem to have been modest. Late Soviet fish was above all marine fish.

Expansion of the catch (in 1975 it was 10.3 million tonnes) went in step with marketing to consumers. One of William Pokhlyobkin's first columns for *Nedelya* assured its readers that flounder and other tender types of white fish 'can accurately be called the chicken of the sea'. It mixed excursions into the past (a century ago, everyone had eaten fish regularly) with advice. Fish should be cooked in enamel dishes (readily available at the time from any houseware shop). An excellent sauce could be made from ordinary processed cheese. In other words, fish brought a quickly prepared, tasty meal within the reach of all.

Fish-eating was promoted not only in the home. A law of 26 October 1976 reintroduced 'Fish Thursdays' for public catering establishments. Specialist fish restaurants, such as Demyan's Fish Soup in Leningrad, began to open their doors.[8] But it was changes to retailing that had the biggest impact. In 1972 came the launch of a nationwide chain of branded supermarkets, 'Okean', with tanks of live fish and counters for filleting and trimming the fresh product, abundant cold storage and attractive tiled interiors, as well as shelf after shelf of tinned and preserved seafood. By 1978, there were over 100 'Okean' stores. The opening of each new branch (Dushanbe, Novosibirsk, Togliatti, Izhevsk, Minsk, etc.) was celebrated in the Soviet press. Mikoyan's model was capitalist America, but Aleksandr Ishkov allegedly got his inspiration from a trip to Franco-era Spain.[9]

In 1977, a journalist for *Izvestiya*, the favourite newspaper of the mainstream Soviet intelligentsia, pointed to the chain as a model for specialist stores providing quality goods. 'Tastings are regularly organised, and selling exhibitions, meetings with chefs and dieticians. The expansion of branded retailing has had a marked impact on the range of fish and seafood on sale, the improvement of packaging. Advertising has acquainted buyers with new, little-known, gifts of the ocean.' Pamela Davidson, a British literary historian and gastronome who spent over a year living in Moscow at this period, was impressed with Okean. So too were many Muscovites. Antonina Z., a keen cook, visited Okean in 21 April 1972 and bought 'fish and tins with an original label' to send a friend in Leningrad; she regularly dropped into the store afterwards. Yuliya Nelskaya-Sidur, on the other hand, recorded on 23 April 1973 how her mother and aunt, 'after queuing for ages', had presented her with cranberries, apples and Hungarian sandals for her small son – but kept the herring from Okean themselves.

If buyers were happy to visit the new stores, the issue for Okean's managers, and Soviet retailing generally, was how to move from 'acquainting' the Soviet population with new products to encouraging enthusiastic purchase of these. In some cases, efforts seem to have been successful. Relentless promotion of 'Ocean Paste', a nutritious spread made of krill, at least familiarized the substance, while 'crab sticks' (manufactured in the USSR from 1984) became positively popular.[10] More adventurous Soviet cooks were happy to try their hand at preparing squid, sold (like many types of ocean fish) with its guts inside and untrimmed. Yet the very success of Okean stores also made them flagships of shortages. Why were no fish and caviar available, even at top prices, wondered a Leningrader in 1975.[11] 'Even in Alma-Ata's biggest fish store, Okean, you cannot always buy cod, hake, and sea perch. The assistants tell you they have nowhere to store the fish because the chillers aren't working', an indignant local wrote to *Pravda* in the autumn of 1977. Long lines and frustration ('I visited Okean, but with no appreciable results') became the typical experience.

Worse (from the point of view of the Soviet government), Okean soon found itself at the centre of a major corruption scandal. In 1979, an investigative committee of the State Procuracy started to examine evidence of large-scale bribes, profiteering and transfer of currency abroad by the director of the Okean chain and a store manager. The transactions, going right up to Deputy Minister for the Fishing Industry Vladimir Rytov, centred on illicit sales of black caviar. Rytov was shot, and Aleksandr Ishkov, also implicated in the case, was forced into early retirement. The case was carefully kept from the Soviet public (the press instead reported public gratitude to the Party authorities for the opening of new stores). But the 'Fish Affair' underlined how Okean had turned from a method of alleviating shortages to a way of making them worse.

Promotion of new products was not left to the store alone. Fish was given prominence among the many specialist cookbooks flowing from Soviet publishers in the 1970s and 1980s. A typical example was N. I. Brunnek and I. N. Morozova's *Fish Cooking* (1984), which recommended to its readers pâté of cod liver and seaweed, smoked red mullet, seaweed caviar and a whole range of fish butters (pickled anchovy with apple, for instance, or capelin with chopped eggs and spring onion), as well as aubergines and oysters in white wine sauce. But many of the dishes were adaptations of familiar meat dishes, made with any marine species that came to hand: fish balls, fish sausages, seafood in pastry, cabbage leaves with fish stuffing, fish sausage rolls.

By 1984, some branches of Okean had literally nothing on sale apart from tins that no one wanted to buy. The chain started to epitomize the clash between the Khrushchev-era approach, volume is all, and the attempt to 'brand' goods of above-average quality. 'For years we've been told: volume and bulk are what matter', said the head of fish production and new technology in Far Eastern Fish, Vladivostok, in 1986. At the start of the year, Far Eastern Fish had a hundred million unsold tins on its hands. Local waters had plenty of sprats (and Latvian smoked canned sprats were one of the country's most sought-after products) (see Figure 3.2). But the fleets concentrated on other fish.

Figure 3.2 Old Riga brand smoked sprats. 2019. Author photograph.

There were problems with public knowledge too: Alaska pollock was in huge demand among the Japanese, yet Soviet buyers considered it hardly fit for their cats. And after nearly thirty years, the local fleet of factory ships was nearing the end of its life.

Fish demonstrated with embarrassing clarity the two besetting problems of late Soviet retailing: scarcity of what people wanted, and abundance of what they didn't. The old traditions lived on in Russians who were amateur anglers, or inhabited areas with abundant fishing and could avail from seasonal gluts.[12] Yet as of 1985, just 29 per cent of the RSFSR's population lived in rural areas, and those fishing in and around big cities (out at the dacha, say) did not necessarily have access to abundant waters. Fish was more likely to be a party dish than a regular item on the table. This even applied to humble selyodka and smoked mackerel, since both required elaborate filleting (and in the first case, prolonged soaking) before they could be plated.

It is scarcely a surprise that in the post-Soviet period, fish retailing and fish consumption shifted out of all recognition. From a situation where only the less favoured types of tinned fish were abundantly available, customers could now browse impressive ranges of smoked, salted and frozen, as well as canned, products. By the start of the 2000s, the fancier type of Russian supermarket also had an ambitious wet fish counter, with tiger prawns for sale alongside salmon and filleted pikeperch.

Pikeperch was something of a domestic success story, a case where a high-status fish could be made reliably available in good condition by Russian farms. Begun in the Soviet period, it flourished after 1991, once better refrigeration and distribution became available. By the end of the 2010s, work had begun on trying to reform the farming itself, using eco-friendly methods, such as recirculating aqua systems, rather than open cages threatening pollution to local wildlife.[13]

Yet pikeperch was definitely aimed at a premium market, which was typical of locally produced fish and seafood. Some favourite kinds commanded stratospheric prices. In the early 2020s, Beluga caviar, back in the 1980s an affordable, if not always available, treat at 4 roubles per

100-gramme jar, or 4 per cent of the average salary, now cost up to 20,000 roubles, or about 50 per cent of the average salary. Live Kamchatka crab might be relatively 'cheap' at 6000 roubles per 100 grams, but that still made it around ten times the price of premium beef.

All the same, there was plenty on offer for fish-loving consumers, not just in overpriced speciality stores with their tanks of crab but on the shelves of more modest places. Sprats, once so difficult to get, were abundant. Many obstacles to appreciation had now vanished. The beloved selyodka no longer had to be laboriously boned; you could buy it ready to use in tidy vacuum packs. Wet fish was sold in good condition, rather than stale or even reeking. In any remote place where visitors congregated, such as the gates of famous monasteries, local villagers set up stalls selling home-smoked fish. A stunning array of cured fish also graced big city markets, such as Moscow's Novye Cheryomushki.

Admittedly, little of this was home-produced. As of 2020, Russia landed 6 per cent of the world's marine catch (the fifth largest haul globally) and 2 per cent of the world's catch on inland waters (the eleventh largest).[14] However, much of the fish went for export. Conversely, fish for domestic consumption usually came

Figure 3.3 Boy angler, Pereslavl-Zalessky, 2012. Author photograph.

from abroad: deep-water prawns from South-east Asia, sea bass from Mauritius, tilapia from India, salmon from Norway and so on. No wonder that, after countersanctions on produce from the EU and EEA were introduced in 2014, fish was an especially notable constituent of the 'grey economy' sector. Shop signs were imaginative – salmon from land-locked Belarus was an especially notable example – but probably convinced only the most trusting members of the older generation. Certainly, there were some domestic successes: once 'Riga Gold' disappeared, factories in Kaliningrad began marketing tinned sprats. And, of course, home anglers continued to put food on tables, and, as provincial places started to rediscover their roots, a fish feast of the kind that Pushkin had enjoyed nearly two centuries earlier started to be a possible pleasure for travellers along the city's major rivers (see Figure 3.3). If the ordinary role of fish was as boring white protein that rang the changes on battery-raised chicken, it could, at least sometimes, rise to the heights of a celebration.

CHAPTER 4
FOREST AND MOOR

In his nostalgic memoir of childhood before the revolution, *Speak, Memory!*, the writer Vladimir Nabokov recalls that his mother's pursuit of forest fungi was one of the greatest pleasures of life at the family's country estate. This was not foraging in the ordinary sense; the crude search for sustenance was subsumed to the joy of the chase:

> As often happened at the end of a rainy day, the sun might cast a lurid gleam just before setting, and there, on the damp round table, her mushrooms would lie, very colorful, some bearing traces of extraneous vegetation – a grass blade sticking to a viscid fawn cap, or moss still clothing the bulbous base of a dark-stippled stem. And a tiny looper caterpillar would be there, too, measuring, like a child's finger and thumb, the rim of the table, and every now and then stretching upward to grope, in vain, for the shrub from which it had been dislodged.
>
> (*Speak, Memory!* 1969)

As Nabokov emphasized, Elena Nabokova was uninterested in the eventual fate of her quarry out in the kitchen, a part of the house that she (so her son insisted) in any case never visited. An apparently humble activity became, in literary recollection, an engagement with the beauty of nature, not an exploitation of nature's bounty as a resource.

Here, *Speak, Memory!* consciously echoes the ways in which Russian literature written a century earlier depicted the pursuit of game. The quintessential activity of the Russian country gentleman, this was likewise presented as an end in itself. Sometimes, the quarry was not, by any standards, edible (as with the wolf hunt in Tolstoy's

War and Peace). But even when it came to wild birds, the hunting expedition (for writers from Sergei Aksakov and Ivan Turgenev to Anton Chekhov) was the occasion for exploration of the countryside, philosophical chat and admiration of nature. The fate of the prey was left outside the frame.

The rise of hunting as a pastime was associated with a shift from trapping (where the prey's odds of escaping were lower) to shooting. In *Hunting with Dogs* (1810), a compendium of hints on the pursuit of wild things, Vasily Lyovshin based the superiority of the gun on the fact that it turned hunting into an encounter with nature: 'One can enjoy visiting a place well stocked with game in the company of a scent hound, whether in the early morning, or after sunset, visiting the forest edge to shoot at animals as they emerge and retreat.'

Yet despite the view that, to reverse Oscar Wilde, only the unspeakable would pursue the eatable, a range of wild creatures, from bears to bustards, did end up on the Russian table. Some, such as partridge or hazel grouse (ryabchik), had gastronomic fame.[1] Likewise, mushroom hunting was in practice not simply about connoisseurship of the growing fungi but about a search for the species that were most useful for cooking, drying and pickling.

For peasant communities, particularly those in the North, trapping and foraging on marginal land – sour bogs as well as forests and taiga – was an ingrained habit. As an anonymous Englishwoman recorded in 1855: 'In the northern provinces there is a kind of yellow fruit, in shape like a mulberry, called maroshca, which makes an excellent preserve, and is also used medicinally as a remedy for the dropsy. Various wild berries, such as cranberries, bilberries, &c., abound in the forests, and numberless species of mushrooms; of all these they make preserves and pickles, which they use in the long winter-season as a substitute for fresh vegetables.'[2] At bad times, living off fruit, tree-bark and mushrooms became a matter of life and death.

Yet forest creatures (squirrels, foxes, martens) were hunted more for their skins than for food. As in some other traditional cultures (Ireland, for instance) animals such as hares were taboo because of beliefs that they were shapeshifters.[3] Indeed, elk, deer and wild birds were generally left alone by peasant Russians, as opposed to, say, the Inuit and Finno-Ugric populations of the far North.

This did not, however, stop peasant communities from trapping wild birds; there was a ready market among those less pious about custom. Game was widely available in Russian cities before 1917, often sold alongside 'greens', a term that embraced foraged plants as well as those grown in market gardens. Meanwhile, village children might be pressed into service to help with berry-picking: 'The children and the peasant women gather wild strawberries, cherries and kizil plums in sufficient abundance to sell in the market', Stephen Graham observed in the Black Sea resort of Gelendzhik at the start of the 1910s.

Though gentlemen such as those on the pages of Tolstoy and Turgenev's novels might take little interest in the fate of their bag, game appeared regularly in Russian cookbooks. Derzhavin's own note to his 'In Praise of Country Life' commented that gastronomes of the day preferred their game high. But the fact that he needed to explain it suggests that to common sense, this view was alien. Certainly, Elena Molokhovets suggested hanging only pheasant. While she recommended other game birds should be plain roast or braised, she gave a wider range for hazel grouse, including stuffed with anchovy, sardine, and pounded allspice and nutmeg; fried in breadcrumbs with a madeira sauce; baked with smetana; presented as a soufflé, or as a breakfast spread with truffles and parmesan. Evidently, it was less the taste of game than its social cachet that counted. With lesser varieties, the strategy was less to mask any possible 'gamey' flavour with expensive seasonings than to purge the meat with vinegar water or warm milk before cooking in a tenderizing braise.

Another popular solution was to present game cold: Ekaterina Avdeeva, for example, suggested adding it to a chopped vegetable salad or using it in a multi-ingredient galantine.[4] This made it easier to remove lead shot, shattered bone and any meat that had got too high for local tastes. To modern eyes, the inclusion of ryabchik in late nineteenth-century recipes for Salad Olivier (alongside crayfish tails) looks prodigal. However, the origins of the dish may have lain in a prudent exploitation, by the fashionable restaurant that invented the dish, of birds that could not be served whole.

Mushrooms (unless expensive imported truffles were at stake) did not require such elaborate intervention. Contrary to Nabokov's studiedly literary picture, this was a type of wild foodstuff that Russian gentlemen and gentlewomen were happy to gather for culinary purposes. The Scottish physician and botanist Robert Lyall, who lived in Russia for several years in the late 1810s, was deeply struck by the local knowledge of fungi. He noted in his *The Character of the Russians* (1823) the command of terrain, whether 'Birch-woods, or Pine-forests', and the way that some places were renowned for their abundant harvests, year on year. 'Mushrooms are eaten fried, boiled or pickled by all classes of society, and are particularly useful during the fasts, dressed with hemp oil by the peasantry, or with olive oil by the nobility. At the other seasons of the year, the dried, salted and pickled stores are required.'

Lyall listed a large number of different dishes: 'They are fried on hot ashes, or in a frying-pan; they are boiled alone; they are roasted with butter alone, or oftener with butter and Smetana, or sour cream. They also enter into the composition of some puddings and pies.' They could be served as a side dish themselves, or with other vegetables. 'They are excellent when prepared with cutlets and rich sauce, duly seasoned.' They were brought to cities by the waggon-load, and sold at modest prices in markets (in Moscow, particularly Okhotnyi ryad, Hunter's Row). Lyall also included a detailed list of preferred types, with both Latin and Russian common names: the 'ryzhik' (Agaricus deliciosus) was usually boiled, fresh or salted, the 'opyonok' (Agaricus fragilis) used in small pies, 'pestrets' (Agaricus dentatus) only eaten when young, and that rarely; the champignon (Agaricus campestris) 'is not highly esteemed'.[5] Judging by cookbooks and diaries alike, the repertoire remained much the same for the next century and more.

As for berries, Russians of the leisured classes did little purposive gathering, though Matvei Andreev, a servant in the household of the Golubtsov family, noted in 1874 that his employer 'was pleased to eat many lingonberries' during pauses in a day out hunting. Those of means were happy to eat them at table, as well as on the hoof. Wild strawberries, raspberries and cloudberries might be served with sour cream or curd cheese; the more resistant species with lower natural sugar, such as cranberries or lingonberries, were more often turned into soft drinks (a sweetened fruit water called mors), used for kissel (a compote thickened with potato flour), or jellies and jams, or sharp sauces to serve with meat (in the combination loved all over Northern Europe).

Unlike agricultural products, wild foods underwent only minimal state intervention after 1917. The main change was tighter regulation of access to firearms. Prior to 1917, Russian statute had merely controlled particular practices relating to gun use, rather than ownership as such. Measures passed in the eighteenth century forbade shooting indoors or in residential districts, and bearing arms in public. In 1835, prisoners in Siberian labour camps and exiles were forbidden from owning firearms; over the next few decades followed regulations aimed against other potentially threatening categories, for example, border-dwellers. But hunters were specifically exempted from prohibition by, for instance, the Rural Police Code on State Peasants (1839), which allowed 'those pursuing wild animals and hunting' to own guns.

From 1903, gun owners had to obtain a licence from the city or provincial governor, while gun shops had to keep records of sale. Still, little attention was paid to firearms used for hunting. Even a statute passed after the uprisings of spring and summer 1905 exempted these from the requirement that governors and mayors should monitor arms sales and storage in emergency situations.

As for hunting as such, the version of the Criminal Code dating from 1885 included fines for poaching on private, state or crown lands, and for the pursuit of protected species, particularly bison. On the other hand, a set of rules promulgated in 1892 allowed hunting on private land by permission of the landowner, and on lands owned by the Ministry of State Properties upon purchase of a licence. At the cost of three roubles (then nearly a third of a city servant's monthly income), this was aimed at the comfortably off, who were also represented by the memberships of the many hunting societies formed at this period. But the 1892 rules did also include provision for the peasants of Arkhangelsk Province, north-eastern Vologda Province, and some districts of Perm and Vyatka provinces, to hunt right round the year – a measure that recognized the importance of hunting to the fragile rural economy – though sales of game were prohibited between 10 March and 1 July. While hunting retained its aristocratic associations, it became more socially accessible in the early twentieth century, as firearms became cheaper and members of hunting societies pressed for broader rights to practise their sport.

The nationalization of land in November 1917 made hunting, at least implicitly, legal in every part of Soviet Russia. It took a little time for detailed regulations to be set in place. While a 1919 law recognized the general right to hunt, another passed on 20 July 1920 made membership of a 'hunters' union' the requirement for obtaining a permit – which automatically also carried entitlement to ownership of a shotgun and ammunition. Permits were provided free of charge, and until 1926, hunting was not subject to any other charges either. Institutional authority was vested in the Hunting Section of the Agricultural Ministry.[6]

Unionization extended not just to issuance of permits but also to practical management of hunting. The Central Cooperative Union of Hunters (Vsekootkhozsoyuz) acted as a source of guns and ammunition, and at the same time an outlet for sales of the hunter's booty – fur, down, horn and leather, but also meat. Effectively, a barter system was in operation – hunters received equipment (as well as cash payments) in return for supplying the Union with game. Though the use of cooperatives as outlets for distribution was widespread in the 1920s, the products of hunting were unique in that cooperatives effectively constituted a monopoly (a situation that continued throughout the rest of Soviet history). Game sometimes appeared in state shops, but that was not the norm.

In the first pre-revolutionary years, game, so far from being a luxury food, started to cost less than some staples. Alexandre Benois recalled that in April 1923, ryabchik could be had for eight 'lemons' (i.e. million-rouble notes in the inflated currency of the time; by comparison, the going rate for a kilo of bread was 14.4 'lemons'). Sardonically he remarked that it was 'now the cheapest of all national delicacies'.

This decline in game's market value and social standing was also reflected in later government policy. In 1933, the Central Cooperative Union of Hunters was shut down, and emphasis shifted to the marketing of fur, largely because of its high export value. Hunting societies went into a decline. All the same, game occasionally reached the market, though it was not always appreciated. On 13 January 1940, writer Mikhail Bulgakov's wife Elena complained to her diary about the ghastly meal the two had endured at the House of Littérateurs, including 'dreadful' game patties for her.

Government interest in game resurfaced during post-war reconstruction. An article published in *Pravda* on 19 July 1947 described meat from game as 'no less important than fur', and advocated the re-creation of a central state management organ (non-existent since 1939) that might offer support to hunters in areas such as dog-breeding and training, and at the same time ensure conservation of wild animals ('pests' such as wolves aside). Yet such an organ was not created till 1954, and in any case, hunters' unions and the Central Cooperative Union (Tsentrosoyuz), now the delegated liaison body, continued to manage both the process of catching game and the mechanisms for marketing it.

Game remained easy to obtain and plentiful throughout the Soviet period. In fact, the main issue was trying to get the Soviet public (aside from those who themselves hunted and their families, or people who obtained game by from hunters they knew) to eat it. Despite suggestions in *The Book of Tasty and Nutritious Food* that ryabchik could be added to salads, the bird now had the status of rabbit during British wartime rationing: obtainable, but lacking in popular appeal. It did not help that the best areas for hunting were remote, with poor access to transport and none to refrigeration. Just as in the nineteenth century, this made winter the practicable season for marketing game – yet in the winter, professional hunts preferred to hunt fur-bearing animals, which brought a far better profit.

Despite further attempts to encourage hunting in the Khrushchev and Brezhnev eras, and the rebranding of cooperatives as 'Gifts of Nature' (or 'Forest Life') shops (see Figure 4.1), the public hesitancy persisted. 'They sold those wild ducks, but they weren't worth it – not much meat on them, feathers everywhere, and quite a price too. Tough, with bits of shot in them', a Siberian recalled.[7] 'My friend's husband used to hunt himself, and if you cook game properly it's delicious, but

Figure 4.1 The Gifts of Nature shop on Komsomol Avenue, Moscow, 1966. *Nasha Rodina SSSR, Vkontakte,* https://vk.com/wall-155870848_586353. Accessed 7 November 2022.

if you bought it frozen in a co-op, people didn't know what to do. One big heap of feathers.'[8] Hunting itself could be immensely prestigious (it was a favourite with Party high-ups across the socialist bloc). Its results did not have the same cachet.

A further blow to the appeal of game was the increasing interest in conservation that began spreading through Soviet society in the 1960s. On 23 August 1967, during the hunter's favourite month, *Literary Gazette* published an article by staff correspondent Vladilen Travinsky, 'The Last Hare', which identified a catastrophic decline in the numbers of game animals across the USSR. Travinsky traced the crisis to the popularity of recreational hunting. In Ukraine alone, for example, local hunting societies now had over 400,000 members, a figure that outstripped by some way the total numbers of all game animals in the republic. A law of 11 May 1959 had imposed on hunting societies the requirement to run game breeding stations, but the results were almost invisible, since half the birds and animals raised were simply used as quarry for shooting. Travinsky proposed a blanket ban on shooting and on the use of vehicles for hunting;

instead, more sporting weapons such as bows and arrows should be used. The vast postbag that resulted, some indignant hunters aside, was largely made up of letters agreeing with Travinsky. *Literary Gazette*'s editorial board rounded off the lengthy exchange with a contribution by veteran author Leonid Leonov, and the deputy minister of forestry for Belorussia, Vladimir Romanov, both of whom lent their authority to Travinsky's case. The hunters defended themselves by blaming irresponsible behaviour on poachers. But as Romanov pointed out, many of those were members of hunters' societies who flagrantly ignored the rules.

For the educated city-dwelling public, game had been dubiously palatable in any case; now it had an aura of cruelty and wastefulness also. The Soviet press continued to publish anti-hunting coverage in the 1970s and 1980s as well, despite (or because of) the sport's popularity with members of the Party elite.

Among other 'gifts of nature', some were consumed only at times of desperation. When Anna Akhmatova referred to her own poetry as 'burdock' and 'orache' in a famous poem from the cycle 'Craft Secrets', written in 1940, she meant something vital in hard times, yet undervalued. The metaphor was exact. Even during the Siege of Leningrad, foraging had a limited hold on everyday practices, despite attempts to encourage it. An exhibition of 'vegetable substitutes' in the Leningrad Botanic Garden in late spring 1942 included 'nettle, deadnettle, goutweed, cow parsnip, wild chervil, plantain, shepherd's purse, orache, wintercress, sow thistle, clover, and even dandelion'. There were also story boards 'showing you how to make cow parsnip or nettle soup, dandelion leaf puree, wild chervil stew, goutweed or shepherd's purse salad'.[9] Some of these plants had occasionally been eaten in Russia, but dandelion (relished in France) was, as in Britain, often thought to be 'poisonous' because of its white sap. Others also accorded poorly with conventional tastes. In June 1942, a cook working in a Leningrad canteen reported to a public meeting that her best success with orache (which flourished in the canteen's yard) had been with pickling the stalks, then using them for soup. The leaves were just too bitter.[10]

Berries, though, retained their hold, sometimes with the direct support of the Soviet state. On 24 July 1933, a mass collection of berries was organized in the new Soviet city of Magnitogorsk, then a vast building project. State agents concentrated their interest on lingonberries and cranberries, which, alongside their antiscorbutic qualities, were easy to pack and transport, given their tough skins. Cranberries had the additional advantage that they were relatively easy to harvest (this could be done mechanically once their bogland habitat froze over). They were also well-suited to industrial processing, as extracts, drinks and syrups.[11] Bilberries, on the other hand, were not commercially grown, though they were sometimes sold through the cooperative network or at markets.

In the post-war decades, as trips outside the city became easier to arrange, and Russians acquired an exurban foothold in the form of a dacha, people were able to gather wild fruit on their allotment, or indeed to plant fruit-bearing bushes. Widespread were rowan, chokeberry ('black rowan' – though the two plants are not related), the fruit of the snowball tree (kalina), sea buckthorn and wild kizil plums. All were hardy and produced abundant fruit. Ways of using them varied. Only ripe chokeberry was pleasant to eat raw; kalina, added to vodka, was popular mainly as a folk antiscorbutic, while sea buckthorn, wild plum and, to a lesser extent, rowan were all popular for syrups and jams.

Russians also remained avid gatherers and eaters of wild mushrooms. Indeed, the taste for these was sometimes wrongly thought to be unique to the nation. Mushroom-gathering was encouraged in state-provided food advice: for instance, *The Book of Tasty and Nutritious Food* had an attractively illustrated essay on edible species. But mainly, expertise circulated in the community itself, with older relations showing children what to pick; in time, the latter passed their lore on to the next generation. As a result, what people considered edible varied from region to region (northerners were by tradition unusually fastidious, perhaps because their historic dependence on mushrooms meant that 'doubtful' species, consumed in bulk, had deleterious effects and were then shunned).[12] At the same time, there was a universal canon of prized species, with Boletus edulis ('white mushroom') at the top, followed by morel ('sticky mushroom', smorchok), chanterelle ('little foxes'), milkcap (gruzd) and a host of lesser species (see Figure 4.2).

Figure 4.2 Basket of boletus mushrooms, Leningrad Province, 2008. Author photograph.

Mushrooms and berries were ingrained in Russian tradition, perhaps more than any other food. Their sale through the cooperative system at first sight seems counter-intuitive. But as the numbers able to visit woodland on the fringes of cities increased, so sought-after wild plants retreated – in part because of indiscriminate harvesting, and in part because of habitat disappearance. The yield dropped off even in some remote places: Galina Zaitseva, visiting Arkhangelsk Province in 1972, was able to pick a generous yield of berries, but in the same place a decade later, even fruit of last resort, such as crowberries, was scarce.[13] During thin times, or if they had to spend the whole summer in the city (not everyone could afford a dacha, or even a holiday), people were grateful for the chance to enjoy traditional foraged food.

Berries and mushrooms were seldom the subject of serious shortages when it came to retail, because there was no expectation they would be there. Cranberries were the exception. Produced by state-owned enterprises, they were subject to the same expectations of availability as, say, milk or eggs – and to the same panic buying, as Yuliya Nelskaya recorded on 20 April 1973:

> Today I visited the stores on Komsomol Avenue [in the prosperous south-west of Moscow]. Like any authentic Soviet citizen living on the principle 'grab what you can, or it'll melt away', I headed straight for the cranberries in polythene bags (they vanished a while back, and Dima really misses them). I snatched ten whole bags, and paid for my greed right away. [...] Three of the polythene bags with cranberries got torn and started dripping juice. I bolted for my studio like a scalded cat, cranberry juice pouring everywhere, and concerned passers-by kept shouting that I'd got a leak. Eventually, I had to stop and (oh horror!) throw out my tins [of cocoa], then set off again with my soggy, sticky string bags, without even worrying about why I wasn't in the crazy lines for horseradish sauce in mayo jars. God, will these lines ever vanish?

It reads like farce, but in real life such incidents were deeply demoralizing.

In the post-Soviet period, the status of 'nature's gifts' was contradictory. Intense interest in 'natural' produce, without preservatives or factory treatment, made hunting and foraging attractive. But there was also much greater awareness than in the Soviet period of the pollution risks (for instance, radiation) that might affect areas of apparently pristine wilderness. Interest in the defence of wildlife had also sharpened. Already in 1995, a law 'On the Animal World' gave absolute protection to endangered species.[14] Unlike his Soviet predecessors, Vladimir Putin took an intense interest in wildlife projects such as saving the Siberian tiger. But hunting remained popular among lower tiers of the elite, and by the start of the 2020s, protection for wildlife had begun eroding again.[15] Not more than 2 per cent of the population hunted regularly, but some of them had significant leverage. You could now buy deer and antelope meat pre-prepared – smoked, tinned, finely sliced for carpaccio – but at extremely high prices (four times the cost of prime beef). Oven-ready ryabchik cost the same as grouse in London. Just as before 1917, to eat game in quantity you needed to hunt yourself, or enjoy a substantial income – or both at the same time.

Berries and mushrooms were often still the preserve of traditional grannies (and occasional grandpas) with jam-jars, or locals with buckets meeting long-distance trains. But the commercial sector had made inroads here too. Brokers scouted rural areas where job opportunities were limited, buying berries from the local population, then selling them on for substantial profits. A more novel development was the emergence of specialist nurseries dedicated to berry production. The majority concentrated on cultivated species (particularly strawberries), but a few were now growing wild or wild-analogue types (in particular, wild strawberries and sea buckthorn berries). The produce could be found in ambitious groceries and even some supermarkets – alongside, rather than instead of, the tropical fruit and hothouse salad vegetables. Yet to a significant extent foraged foods, unlike game, continued their existence as foods beyond the reach of the state or even the market, and in greatest abundance in precisely the areas most remote from city life.

CHAPTER 5
GARDEN AND ORCHARD

'Cabbage', wrote Charles Stoddard, an American visitor to Russia in 1892, 'may almost be considered as national in Russia as the potato is in Ireland'. Indeed, there are few other countries where a major poet might pay tribute to a fine juicy cabbage as the ornament of patriotic cuisine.[1] Brassica oleracea was long considered the revenge of heaven on Britain, and the metallic stench of overcooked leaves is a traumatic recollection of many born before 1970. For Russians, though, it was the most tolerant of vegetables (growing across most of the empire), and the most versatile. Salted, pickled, stewed with meat for delicious shchi or with oil and other vegetables for a Lenten version; soaked in butter and mixed with hard-boiled eggs for a pie filling; shredded in salads; wrapped round minced meat to produce 'little pigeons' … the variety is stunning.

Even in pampered St Petersburg, cabbage was by far the most important crop in local market gardens, as a 1914 survey by Nikolai Kichunov made clear. Yet access only to cabbage was considered a deprivation. Ekaterina Avdeeva observed that even in Siberian cities such as Tyumen and Irkutsk, people grew a wide variety of vegetables, sowing cucumber, cabbage and pumpkin seedlings in early May 'in hotbeds with sides of planking, and at the end of May, they transplant what they have sown into the ground'. In the south-west of the country, both vegetables and fruit grew abundantly. Visiting Kursk, Avdeeva noted that almost every home had its orchards. As well as many varieties of apples and pears, plums, cherries sweet and sour, currants, gooseberries and raspberries, locals grew berberis and even bergamot. Fruit was dried, used to make kvas and served as a relish with meat dishes, as well as a dessert at the meal's conclusion. In Ukraine, the variety of vegetables and fruits was still greater, both home-produced and imported into the Russian Empire's biggest southern port, Odesa.[2] Alongside cabbage, and other staples such as onions, carrots, and beetroot, St Petersburg's early twentieth-century commercial gardeners could offer round and long types of lettuce, sorrel, chicory, and even scorzonera.

Cookbooks from nineteenth- and early twentieth-century Russia reflected this abundance, giving much space to the preparation and cooking of 'greens', 'roots' and 'vegetables' generally.[3] The many fasts meant that vegetable dishes might graduate to mains. But even on meat and milk days, vegetable side dishes were common (a few pickles with your roast, perhaps), and green salads (served, as in France or England of the day, with or after the entrée) were also popular.[4] As cities expanded, and market gardens proliferated round their fringes, the authors of cookbooks started to fret that eating raw vegetables might be risky: in *The Practical Principles of the Vegetarian Table* (1914), Aleksandra-Ignatyeva warned of possible sewage contamination even if thoroughly washed. But 'salad' in Russia had in any case always also meant mixtures of chopped cooked vegetables (such as vinegret, comprising potatoes and beetroot).

As the case of the potato suggested, vegetables were important not just for health, variety and refreshment but also for sustenance. Potatoes were already well-established in the urban 'middle state' by the middle of the nineteenth century: 'Like the English, the Russians take potatoes with nearly every dish – either plain boiled, fried, or with butter and parsley over them', reported Henry Sutherland Edwards in 1861. Yet even a decade later, there were areas of peasant Russia where the potato was deeply alien; some believed it was shaped like a man and could bleed, others that potatoes were 'devil's eggs', and that mice hatched out of them. However, the close ethnographical evidence collected by informants for the Tenishev Bureau in the early 1890s suggests very effective assimilation in some areas. 'Without the potato, most of the population would starve, especially in the spring and the early summer', came the report from Sogalich District in Kostroma Province.[5] 'Thirty years ago, the use of potatoes was almost unknown to local peasants', an informant from Yaroslavl Province commented.

'But now potatoes are pretty well the most important constituent of the local diet.'[6]

There was still at least a limited place in the diet for older staples. Split peas, mentioned in the *Domostroi*, retained importance as a food crop. In the Vladimir area, painter Vasily Vereshchagin saw the elaborate work that went into their preparation: they were 'scalded, then [...] dried three times over – and here great care is to be taken that the peas do not get yellow and lose their green colour. If they turn yellow, they will immediately come down in price'. Eating peas before they were dried was the prerogative of naughty children drafted to help with the shelling. Dried peas not sold might be 'boiled with butter or oil and onion', turned into a gruel or used for pie fillings, or 'something resembling pease sausage'.[7]

Buckwheat, grecha, also mentioned in the *Domostroi* (the word itself signifies 'Greek', betraying foreign origins), was used in similar ways, though some people had started mixing it with wheat, or indeed using wheat products instead, when prices allowed.[8] It was more tenacious as a porridge, served with milk on holidays.[9]

The widespread use of vegetables in the traditional Russian diet did not necessarily generate enthusiasm. The association of meat and milk with celebration made their absence seem punitive. Hence the readiness of Russians who had perforce abstained to alter their habits when they arrived in cities. By and large, principled vegetarianism was the prerogative of people who were privileged at least in the sense that they were highly educated. Leo Tolstoy, one of the movement's most influential figures, was one example, Natalia Severova-Nordman another.[10] Yet the movement gained traction precisely among educated Russians in the early twentieth century, as the appearance of various specialist cookbooks indicated.

The most impressive of these was *I Don't Eat Anyone!* (1913) by 'A Vegetarian Lady', the pseudonym of Olga Zelenkova. From a Russified Ukrainian family with estates in Chernihiv Province, 100 miles north of Kyiv, she was the daughter of a senator, and the sister of high-ranking civil service official and part-time poet Konstantin Sluchevsky. Zelenkova's book was a remarkably thorough and imaginative guide to eating without meat. It opened with a seasonal calendar, providing a detailed list of vegetables available in a given month:

> **JANUARY.** Swede. – Jerusalem artichoke – Parsley. – White cabbage, red cabbage, brussels sprouts. Chestnuts. Cress. Parisian market carrots [short round ones]. Potatoes. Sweet roots [parsnip, celeriac]. Green onion, Spanish onion, bulb onion, shallot. Beetroot. Young beets. Round lettuce, Romaine, chicory. Ground elder. Soup asparagus. Radish. Mustard leaves. Narva turnip. Cultivated mushrooms. Spinach. Sorrel.

The simple recipes (such as beet and cress salad, cooked vegetables with a sauce made from beaten egg yolks with lemon juice, salt, sugar and chopped herbs, or Parisian market carrots and sugar peas in jelly) were designed to show off fresh seasonal produce. The book had run to three editions, the second of 7000 copies, by 1917.

All the same, it took the deprivations of the post-revolutionary period for meatless eating to move, temporarily as it turned out, into the mainstream. Olga Merezhkovskaya's recipes for émigré readers still made extensive use of (economy-priced) cuts of meat. But they also borrowed extensively from the French tradition of light, puréed vegetable soups using milk as a thinner, and dishes such as céleri rémoulade. In the USSR, the promotion of vegetables went considerably further. During the 1920s, specialized institutes began working extensively on the formation of seed banks, with the result that the country became a world leader in this area (Russia still has unparalleled stocks of traditional vegetable types).

There was also attention to culinary advice. Brochures and magazines for the mass market (such as *Working Woman*) reworked well-known dishes in new versions: marrows or peppers stuffed with a meatless filling, rather than mince, for example. The guidance was accompanied by information on the health benefits of a plant diet, drawing extensively on recent scientific discoveries about the significance of vitamins. Members of the Soviet 'middle state' also took a new interest in healthy salads: Mikhail Prishvin noted on 11 July 1930 a recipe for a spring salad comprising fresh cucumber chopped along with fresh radishes and potato, then dressed with vinegar.

This ethos of simplicity and restraint underwent a radical shift in the Stalin era. Now, vegetables were no longer substitutes for meat (which, in theory at least, was supposed to be on every Soviet table), but ancillary to it. The word 'salat', rather than meaning a dish that followed an entrée as a kind of palate-refresher, started to mean something much more substantial. The Americanization of Soviet meat production was followed by the Americanization of the salad.

Compared with frankfurters, the arrival of the new type of salad was a little delayed. The first edition of *The Book of Tasty and Nutritious Food* included a selection of salads in mayonnaise, some with meat as an ingredient alongside chopped vegetables (as in the classic American chicken salad). These were 'most often served as a zakuska at the beginning of dinner, supper, lunch, or breakfast'. However, it also included compositions of raw vegetables like those served before 1917, among them, such esoteric (in the Russian context) leaves as Romaine lettuce and endives. It was the 1952 edition that gave the salad made with bottled mayonnaise dominance of the zakuska table.

The Stalinist salad ('stalad', one might say) did not have to contain meat. *BTNF* 1952, for instance, included a salad of chopped lettuce, hardboiled eggs, and sour cream and a vinegret with chopped vegetables and fruit. However, the quintessential 'stalad' provided a showcase for the luxury foods of the new era. 'Meat Salad', for example, comprised 200 grams of meat, 4–5 potatoes, 2 cucumbers, 100 grams of chopped lettuce and half a glass of bottled mayonnaise. A vinegret with 'conserved meat' was made with a tin of stew, 5–6 boiled potatoes, 3 salted cucumbers, 1 boiled beetroot, 100 grams of green onion, 1 or 2 eggs, half a glass of mayonnaise, a teaspoonful of mustard and a serving spoon of vinegar. There were also salads with chopped sausage, with ham, and with tinned crab.[11]

An important feature of the 'stalad' was that its main vegetable components (potatoes, carrots, cucumbers) were those readily available through the state supply system. Lettuce and other green leaves are fragile and spoil easily; they are best grown and marketed by specialists of the kind who had ceased to exist at the end of NEP.

Green leaves were also a problem for the cook: they required careful washing, but not all Soviet citizens, even in cities, had easy access to clean running water. Cooked chopped vegetables were a practical recourse; a garnish of sausage or crab made use of ingredients with a long shelf life to dress them up for a party. The pinnacle among such salads was Salad Olivier, a very different animal from the pre-revolutionary salad known by that name. Now made with chicken, not game, and no crayfish, this was lifted to party status by the inclusion of bottled peas, and of course a dressing of bottled mayonnaise as well. Such salads were in reality not necessarily healthy – they could be indigestible and harbour microbes.[12] But they at least appeared to combine the 'tasty' and 'healthy' categories evoked in the nation's principal cookbook. Raw vegetable mixtures such as 'salat Vitaminnyi' never had the same cachet.

A related development of the Soviet era was the popularization of the tomato. Cookbooks of the nineteenth century had presented it as an exotic luxury. Radetsky's *Almanac for Gastronomes* (1855) included tomatoes stuffed 'à la provençale'. Odoevsky's Doctor Puf, using the fancy term, 'pommes d'amour', claimed they were 'essential for sauces' and suggested bottling them. But only a few of his own recipes actually used tomato. The earliest reference to tomatoes in the vast Prozhito.ru database of diaries is from 1891.[13]

Kichunov's 1914 study of Petersburg market gardens confirms that they began to be grown in significant quantities in the early 1890s. By the 1900s, the capital's premier grower, D. F. Feofanov, had tens of thousands of plants on his holding at Ligovo, about half an hour away by rail. He was also a successful breeder, who had developed a near-seedless version of the tomato, elegantly spherical and with smooth skin. Tomatoes were planted out in late May, picked green, and ripened in special glasshouses, known as 'zorilki', or 'blush houses', so they turned the requisite scarlet (see Figure 5.1). Only in the depths of winter and early spring were buyers reliant on tomatoes imported from Algeria and Madeira. Diaries of the period confirm the ready market for tomatoes: the Benois family used them for macaroni sauce, while other families put them in pickles, served them chopped and stewed as caviar, or simply ate them raw.[14]

Рис. 244. Сборъ томатъ съ грядъ передъ осенними утренниками.

Figure 5.1 Tomato gathering in D. F. Feofanov's market garden. Nikolai Kichunov, *Market Gardening and Commercial Berry-Growing Outside Petrograd*, 1914.

Once healthy eating went mainstream, the tomato's high content of vitamins, particularly A and C, raised its prominence.[15] In her 1928 brochure, *Learn to Cook Well*, Marina Zarina listed it among 'essential seasonings', along with salt, sugar, vinegar, mustard, onion, garlic, horseradish, pepper and bay leaves. Particular attention was given to preserving, given that the maximum keeping time was just five weeks, even refrigerated. *Salting Tomatoes*, a brochure published in 1933 by the All-Soviet Cooperative Association, provided elaborate instructions for grading tomatoes by State Standard 2906, making brine, and flavouring it with bayleaf, tarragon and hot pepper ('basil is also permitted'; other recipes suggested hyssop, dill and marjoram too). The intent was a neutral product, not one fermented according to traditional practice. 'No gases should escape when the barrels are opened.'

In the second half of the 1930s, tomatoes were quite widely grown in southern areas of the USSR. Nikolai Ustryalov, then a consultant on the Chinese-Eastern Railway, approvingly called them 'the truffles of the modern Georgian table' when he saw them growing in the Caucasus on 12 August 1936. They also featured in the 1939 edition of *The Book of Tasty and Nutritious Food*, listed among high-vitamin foods. I. P. Tsyplyonkov's humbler 1939 cookbook of '200 dishes for the family kitchen' included salads with tomato.[16] The narrator of Viktor Nekrasov's 1946 novel *In the Trenches of Stalingrad* was struck by the 'mountains of cucumbers and tomatoes' at the city bazaar in September 1942. By the 1950s, a salad of sliced cucumber and tomato had become a staple of Soviet canteens. In the Khrushchev era, tomato paste – originally manufactured as a way of using up harvest gluts – was assiduously promoted to the Soviet public. *Kulinariya*, the flagship mass catering textbook of 1955, suggested adding it, among other things, to borshch recipes, and lamb with prunes.[17] Unlike sweetcorn, tomato paste took off – to the extent that by the late 1960s, it was one of the foods subject to sudden shortages.[18]

Fresh tomatoes were difficult to get hold of – and expensive. In Russian cities, ripe, juicy, sweet ones were reliably available only from collective farm markets, at corresponding prices. Not surprisingly, they were a popular crop on the dachas and allotments that also proliferated during the Khrushchev era. The central purpose of allocating these smallholdings had in fact been to increase food production: according to the rules, failure to cultivate one's plot could lead to confiscation. The rules were not strictly enforced, but many people grew at least some vegetables, or failing that, used the dacha for pickling and storing bought ones.

A more fundamental salad vegetable was the ridge cucumber (ogurets) (see Figure 5.2). This had arrived centuries before the tomato (the *Domostroi* mentions it, for instance), and was far more widely eaten. Not all peasant communities grew cucumbers: in parts of Yaroslavl Province, it was customary to purchase them from local landowners.[19] But some market-gardening areas were famous for their cucumbers. The Ukrainian town of Nizhyn (or Nezhin), where writer Nikolai Gogol went to school, still has a monument to the 'Nizhyn cucumber' ornamenting its main street.[20] Cucumbers provided a welcome crunch in a diet of mainly soft food. They were refreshing in summer, and though fresh cucumbers rot fast in warm weather, they can be stored long term if cured. The favourite treatment was brine, with sufficient levels of salt to slow, rather than inhibit, fermentation. Many other vegetables, and indeed fruits, were also brined (garlic, tomatoes, apples, plums and cabbage), but cucumbers were the most popular – flavoured with a selection of leaves (oak, blackcurrant, cherry, horseradish, bay, among others) as well as the dill.[21] At the same time, fresh cucumbers were also widely used when available.

As well as dachas, the post-Stalin years were also a boom time for vegetable-growing on the private plots allocated to collective farmers. Under Stalin, a punitive tax regime had acted as a disincentive.[22] The official attitude shifted in the next decades from semi-prohibition to

Figure 5.2 Radish and cucumber salad, *Kulinariya*, 1955. Although fussily styled, this is a simple chopped fresh vegetable mixture with sunflower oil and vinegar.

active encouragement. Kolkhoz markets were remarkable exhibitions of fresh, varied and delicious produce, at the far end of the continuum from the often wilted and mould-speckled vegetables sold in state outlets. Fresh and pickled cabbages, cucumbers, and garlic; marrows and pumpkins in season; dill, basil, lovage, celery leaves; lettuces, sorrel and spinach, heaps of sunflower seeds, their husks still on – the vegetable stalls were the heart of the market. Alongside bounty from local plots would be heaps of tomatoes and aubergines from the south – including the Caucasus and Central Asia as well as the Kuban and Ukraine. The markets had a celebratory air, a function of their price, though herbs were by any standards cheap; a whole bunch cost less than bread.

As for fruit, before 1917, commercial production stretched across a wide area of central and southern Russia, Ukraine and the Caucasus, including the holdings of some traditional landowners (the real-life equivalents of Chekhov's Lyubov Ranevskaya and her cherry orchard), small producers in cities such as Kursk and Tula, who particularly specialized in apples and pears, and villagers in the areas round the Black Sea. At Gelendzhik in the early 1910s, Stephen Graham observed 'russet pears green speckled, rusty brown and purple grapes'. He also saw blackberries, 'large and sweet wild grapes', and walnuts growing wild; in some villages apples grew so freely that people fed them to the pigs. The southern reaches of the Russian Empire were also the home of an increasingly active wine-making industry, including not just the millennia-old production in Georgia and Armenia but French-type wines in Crimea and Bessarabia.

Planners of the Stalin era hoped not just to raise fruit production in these established areas but also to exploit more distant territories. Eighty per cent of the fruit harvest in Turkestan was used only locally, commented the 1928 edition of *Marketing Food Products*. The aim was to tap such further reaches of empire. The next edition of the book, published in 1933, took the idea further. Fruit trees could grow in severe climatic conditions, as well as more favourable ones, it proclaimed. Siberia, for example, could become a centre of production. New cities should have their own growing facilities. At the moment, average consumption in the USSR was just 10 kilos a head per annum. By 1937, it should be raised to 100 kilos per annum.

Real-life achievements fell short: there were no orange plantations on the Altai, or melons in clearings round Leningrad. Consumption, outside areas where fruit was plentiful and cheap, remained low throughout the Soviet period.[23] As cities expanded in size, traditional orchards disappeared with them, and so too the many different kinds of apple and pear, the pride of the localities.

Even in the season, there was at best a limited selection of Russian-produced fruit available for sale. In September, the Voronezh market overflowed with apples (green and knobbly, but less bruised than in the state shops), and buckets of purple plums. Apricots, cherries, figs and peaches, let alone citrus fruit, all came from the southern republics.

Just as grain and meat trading had once benefitted from the development of the railway system, now fruit marketing was helped by the expansion of the Soviet air network. The cost of fares, while not cheap, could be recouped many times by money made on sales – leaving enough left over for visits to restaurants, where market traders were among the highest-spending clients; the purchase for resale of foods and consumer goods that were scarce in the 'periphery' also lined the traders' pockets. The ideological opposition to such 'profiteering' had not died away completely. But retaliation by the authorities was limited to occasional clean-ups on a demonstrative basis. And the traders had enough cash to buy themselves out of trouble if that happened.

Some fruit did make its way into the processing industry. For instance, there was a range of soft drinks that were sold, in three-litre jars, as 'juice' (they were actually a combination of fruit puree and syrup). Moldova in particular had an active canning industry. Yet Soviet commercial preserving was rather unambitious. There was a striking contrast with such successful brands from other socialist countries as Polish Globus or Bulgarian Oberon. Soviet factory-made fruit-based goods – for instance, jam – also tended to be of poor quality compared with home-made.[24] Wine production was likewise more notable for volume than quality, with fortified drinks such as 'portvein' and 'kagor' much easier to obtain than 'dry wine' from Georgia or Armenia.

An indication of fruit's status as 'treat rather than staple' was the lack of concern about shortages. Anything exotic, such as bananas or mandarins (shipped in from the so-called Third World) required a queue, but that didn't prompt letters to the Soviet press. After all, there were always home-preserved berries to rely on. With vegetables, anxieties were closer to the surface. Why were there no onions for sale? ran one of the questions to a Leningrad Communist Party lecturer in the winter of 1975.[25] Potato shortages even reached the pages of *Pravda*, which waxed indignant over a case in April 1982 when a local administration swapped production to nearer the city, but then ran out of potatoes because there was insufficient space for the required yield.

The reason for moving the potato fields in the first place had been the convenience of temporary workers. In a survival from the collective practices of the 1920s, it was customary for members of the city intelligentsia (research staff at institutes, university teachers, students etc.) to be drafted into temporary work for a few days during vegetable harvests. The *Pravda* article treated this situation as normal, indeed desirable. But the existence of the crisis testified that the practice wasn't working well.

At the end of the Soviet period, food shortages reached a pitch when city-dwellers were much readier to participate because getting a share of the crop was essential to the household economy. Particularly for people living in provincial cities, work on allotments became not so much a pleasant holiday pastime as a condition of survival. This process continued into the early 2000s also (see Figure 5.3). However, the development of Western-style supermarket chains altered vegetable production to the pattern obtaining in the early twentieth century. Polytunnels in the areas immediately outside Moscow and St Petersburg produced mountains of ridge cucumbers for sale in the cities. And just as in the past, the route of the crops to the buyer was indirect – through middlemen and broker companies.

Such broker companies also worked to make good the shortfall of vegetables and fruit once imported from the south-eastern parts of the USSR. It rapidly became cheaper to transport from Turkey or indeed the Canary Islands than from, say, Armenia or Uzbekistan. By 2010, Spanish and Dutch tomatoes, onions, aubergines, citrus fruit, melons and grapes were everywhere in Russian shops. With the imposition of counter-sanctions against the EU, Russia's global networks changed – but by and large (Uzbek melons and tomatoes at premium prices aside), it was mainstream exporters to Western Europe such as Morocco, Israel and South Africa who picked up the slack, alongside Turkey. Just as with 'Belorussian salmon', too, there was evidence of 'secondary export'. For instance, there was a certain St Petersburg shop which, in 2019, purported to be selling grapes and other soft fruit from Yemen. (Even before the devastating civil war, Yemen was almost entirely given over to subsistence agriculture.)

Growing vegetables and fruit is, relative to grain crops, labour intensive, particularly at the initial stages. Population flight to the cities left many rural areas without the pairs of hands needed to sow, weed and bring the crops in. Tied as they were to supermarket rather than specialist distribution, the new market gardens round cities concentrated on the Soviet-era repertoire of cucumbers, potatoes, carrots, onions, pale-green peppers, and of course cabbage. 'Cabbage is God for me', enthused a middle-aged assistant at the Academy of Sciences Library.[26] But twenty-somethings who couldn't remember the USSR didn't regret the disappearance of traditional Soviet 'juice'. Instead, they relished freshly squeezed smuzi (smoothies); and for them, a Greek or Italian salad – lighter and more digestible than the mayonnaise specials – was welcome fare, whether made with local ingredients or those sped to the city by the offices of air freight.

Figure 5.3 Vegetable gardens, Pereslavl-Zalessky, 2012. Author photograph.

CHAPTER 6
HIVE AND REFINERY

In a disturbing scene from Dostoevsky's *The Brothers Karamazov*, sixteen-year-old Liza Khokhlakova tells the novel's protagonist, novice monk Alesha Karamazov, about her fascination with scenes of torture. Reading about a young boy who was first mutilated and then crucified, she identifies with his tormentors: 'I sometimes think it was me that crucified him. He hangs there groaning, and I sit in front of him eating pineapple compote.'

The association of sweet foods and perverted visions echoes the literal meaning of the Russian word for lasciviousness, 'sweet passion' (sladostrastie). Indulgence of the flesh by eating equals sexual indulgence of the flesh. The medieval and early modern Orthodox Church maintained tight control over sexuality; consumption of sweet things was also regulated. The *Domostroi* provided a modest list of home-produced sweets: 'God has sent everything to your home, and you buy nothing; lingonberry water and cherries in patoka, and raspberry mors and all kinds of sweet things, and apples and pears in kvas, and in patoka, and fruit leathers, and pies.'

Patoka in modern Russian is the word for treacle, the dark, sticky by-product of the sugar (or starch-making) industry. In sixteenth- and seventeenth-century Russian, it was the word for honey of the finest quality, poured straight from the comb and with wax carefully removed. As in all European countries, up to the modern era, honey was the primary sweetener for culinary purposes, producing a sense of continuity with biblical tradition. Even after sugar had come into use, honey was used for ritual dishes such as kutya, and for celebration food, such as gingerbread (or honeyed spice cake), pryanik. Honey was widespread as a sweetener in traditional households even during the second half of the nineteenth century. In the Kursk area, for instance, almost every village had a bee-keeper. Lime honey was produced in vast quantities, but the region was also famed for forest honey and meadow honey.

Sugar was first imported into Russia during the late eighteenth century, as an expensive delicacy. From the early 1800s, home production developed. Beet-growing and sugar refineries became favourite forms of landowner entrepreneurship, particularly in southern Russia and Ukraine.[1] Sugar suited the patrimonial calendar because its production was seasonal. The relatively late maturation of sugar beet (in early autumn) left labourers free not just for haymaking and grain harvesting beforehand but for sowing afterwards.

By the 1840s, sugar was a recognized luxury for the 'middle state'. Boris Volzhin's 1842 *Encyclopaedia* paid tribute to the value of the commodity by suggesting that readers keep sugar in a tea-caddy of 'precious wood'. He recommended it for just a dozen or so recipes. Ekaterina Avdeeva's *Pocket Cookbook* (1846) included a bigger variety of dishes in which sugar was used: milk soups, cherry and curd cheese dumplings, sweet drinks with beaten egg whites, steamed or boiled puddings in the English style, fruit jellies, mousses, and creams, poppy seed cake, gingerbread plain and with almonds, and sugared breads. S. Rogalskaya's *The Family Table* (1865) had a longer list (about 180 items in all), but again focusing mainly on kissel, sweet yeasted breads, pies, waffles, jellies, puddings and set creams, though with attention now given to ices also.

Elena Molokhovets's suggestions in the various editions of her book mainly followed this traditional pattern of plain cakes and pies, still further simplified for Lenten fasts. The list of food prices provided in the 1901 edition (pp. iii-iv) provides some background to this. At 16 kopecks per pound or 18 kopecks for best quality refined, sugar cost much the same as top quality beef (18 kopecks), while luxury flavourings such as cocoa (1.18 roubles per pound) and chocolate (60 kopecks to 1 rouble per pound) reached or exceeded the level of chicken (45–65 roubles each), poularde (75 kopecks), and capon (90 kopecks-1 rouble). Not surprisingly, rich confections tended to be occasional purchases from patisseries, for instance, the 'Curaçao-flavoured gâteau' that painter Konstantin Somov brought to poet Mikhail Kuzmin on 2 October 1906.

Prodigality with sugar was the prerogative of the wealthy, like the Abelson family of St Petersburg, whose money came from the lumber business. Sugar figured prominently even at parties for the family's children in the 1910s, as Tamara Abelson, later Talbot Rice, recalled:

> We sat on small chairs around small tables. Our plates and cutlery were also small versions of the dining-room ones. Our meal was served by our servants' older children. Ivan took as much trouble in producing small spun-sugar centre-pieces for my tables as he did over the larger ones required for my parents' banquets.

This was very different from the standard method of consuming sugar among the peasantry and working classes – holding a lump between your teeth as you sipped tea. (In Russian traditional tea-houses, you paid for the sugar, rather than the beverage.) Yet sugar was also eaten widely by the inhabitants of rural areas. 'If they have no honey, they use sugar syrup', recorded one of Prince Vladimir Tenishev's ethnographers in Yaroslavl Province (1898). Another informant in the same province noted that even the poorest families expected to eat about 30 grams per person per day of sugar (middling families would get through about 70 grams, and the richest families closer to 90 grams). On holidays at least, villagers enjoyed a variety of sweet dishes: kissel, gingerbread (usually bought in, rather than baked) and sweetened sour cream with raisins.[2] In some households, vatrushki (open tarts made with bread dough) were baked with curd cheese and treated as a kind of simple pudding.[3]

By the early twentieth century, cookbooks aimed at 'the middle state' had begun to include more ambitious sweet dishes. For instance, A. A. Ryndina's *A Cookbook for Everyone* (1905) included alongside such traditional modest desserts and puddings as mazurka (a simple cake with nuts and/or dried fruit) numerous layered gâteaux. Typical was a 'mocca gâteau' made of fifteen egg yolks, half a pound of sugar and the same of butter, the layers to be soaked in rum-flavoured syrup after cooling and then sandwiched with coffee- and vanilla-flavoured buttercream. Aleksandrova-Ignateva's *The Practical Foundations of the Culinary Art* (1899) also included rich cakes of this kind.

Alongside formal meals, tea provided space for sweet delights. As Elena Molokhovets wrote:

> Sometimes friends assemble for a convivial chat lasting long past midnight, and in such cases late evening tea poured by the lady of the house can even replace supper. This tea is served in the following manner: a long dinner table is set out covered by a clean cloth, and to one side is placed a small table with the samovar. In the middle of the table is put a tall vase of fruits, such as apples, pears, oranges, mandarins and grapes. Along both sides of the vase, across the table, are placed dessert dishes in piles and beside them dessert knives of silver and bone.
>
> To both sides of the vase running down the table are placed long dishes covered with napkins, and in these baking, for instance, white loaves and babas, saffron-flavoured, made of plain wheaten dough, or with almonds, and English and plain biscuits, homemade or bought in.

Served with cherry squash and sherbet as well as rum, red wine and tea itself, the meal was a kind of equivalent to the traditional English dessert of fruit and sweetmeats. Elegance and pleasure were far more important than nutrition. No doubt Russian women from the servant-employing strata of society themselves oversaw the confection of sweet dishes, as happened in British households of the era.

By 1913, Russian production of sugar per annum had reached over 1 million tonnes per annum, significantly above the output of fish or indeed meat. Sweets and candies stood at over 100,000 tonnes per year. The production of sugar was a rare instance in the food world where the Soviet authorities inherited a relatively high-function industrial base. Into the twenty-first century, refineries founded before 1917 made up the backbone of production in some regions.

Sugar availability did not contract right away when the First World War started. The German blockade of the Russian ports released to the home market foods that would usually have been exported. However, by early 1916, hoarding by producers and banks had created shortages and high prices, to popular dissatisfaction.[4] In May 1916, rationing for sugar was introduced: 1 lb per person per month. The amount increased to 3 lb in early 1917, but in the chaos of revolution, the supply situation got far worse. 'There is no sugar. No-one sowed any sugar beet. That really scares me, because I can't live without sugar', Alexandre Benois fretted on 9 June 1917. The ration in July was down to half a pound per person per month. After the October Revolution, the authorities lowered prices by fiat, but shortages persisted. The biggest treat anyone in Moscow or Petrograd could think of was to eat sugar on its own.[5]

Once NEP began, cakes and pastries rapidly reappeared, but, as Vera Shtein noted in her diary on 13 August 1921: 'For the moment we have to content ourselves with shop windows.' Huge crowds massed outside a shop on Nevsky that had just opened, 'and there really was something to look at: two vast coffee and chocolate gâteaux, a sponge cake, pastries, and a vatrushka'. The shop windows may not have encouraged buying, but they seem to have encouraged home baking, at least of a modest kind. Marina Tsvetaeva's sister Anastasiya, for instance, ran up improvised cakes on the standard cooking device of the day, a primus.[6] But by 5 July 1925, supplies of professionally made cakes had increased to a level where the greedy numismatist Aleksei Oreshnikov could nonchalantly tell his diary, 'I bought the prince a gâteau from Muir' (Muir-Merrilies, Moscow's premier department store), as though nothing had changed since 1913. Walter Benjamin's Moscow diary recorded his fascinated repulsion on 1 January 1927 at the 'sickly-sweet flowerbeds' on the tops of Russian gâteaux, and the still more ostentatious ones like horns of buttercream plenty. Soviet Russia was the world's last refuge for the German fancy baker of the past, he concluded.

After the end of NEP, the sugar rush died down. The standard ending to the meal was now kompot, a runny kind of stewed fruit, often made with dried ingredients, served in a glass, which also acted as a rehydrating agent (drinks were not usually served with the meal itself). For instance, a children's menu published in *Working Woman* magazine by Marina Zarina in 1930 concluded with kompot. A gâteau was something truly special: auctioned to raise money for the air club in Barnaul, perhaps.[7]

Matters changed again with the Mikoyan 'gastronomic luxury' drive. Soviet production of ice cream (a long-established pleasure among the Russian moneyed classes) was the pride of the era, and, to judge by diaries, people of the 'middle state' began to eat sweet things quite often.[8] However, even in Leningrad, the elegant former capital, production of patisserie, biscuits, and cakes could be distinctly rough-and-ready. A 1939 inspection of the factory making cakes and sweets for Leningrad's celebrated Café Nord found the floor under the mechanical beaters in the dessert section encrusted with dirt. When the electric mixers in the sponge cake section overflowed, workers would scrape the spillage off the floor and tip it back in.[9]

Sweet things continued to be eaten during the war, but often in transmuted form: a name-day cake made from buttered bread, sugar lumps and berries taken from a liqueur bottle, or 'pastries with albumen filling', or (at less dire times) coarse semolina ground in a coffee mill and baked in a Dutch oven.[10] The daughter of officials at the Ministry of Trade remembered that, in the post-war years, eating white bread was the biggest luxury that she could imagine.[11] Even the 1952 edition of *The Book of Tasty and Nutritious Food* listed only simple dishes such as fruit pies, pancakes, jellies, compotes, biscuits, very simple baked cakes, creams, ice creams and puddings made of fruit and sliced bread (a handy way of using up leftovers).

In the mid-1950s, things began to change. The flagship catering manual, *Kulinariya*, published in 1955, included a resplendent successor to Benjamin's horn of plenty cake (see Figure 6.1).

In the 1955 edition of *The Book of Tasty and Nutritious Food* a luscious colour illustration of a gâteau was accompanied by a credit, 'Bolshevik Factory, Moscow'. Such Soviet-style advertising helped to convince readers that top-quality goods could be obtained in particular places. In later decades, certain star cakes, such as an adaptation of Sachertorte from the Restaurant Prague in Moscow, were trophies for the tireless shopper.[12]

Soviet factories increased the quantity and variety of sweet things available to the Soviet shopper. The production plan for Leningrad's Samoilova Factory in 1956 included not just revived pre-war types of biscuit but also new kinds, as well as novel lines of confectionery

Figure 6.1 Horn of Plenty cake, *Kulinariya*, 1955.

(soft meringue in chocolate, fruit jellies, and catchily-named candies called 'Stratosphere'). The recipes were planned to take advantage of mechanization and new types of additive (for instance, the acidity regulator and preservative sodium lactate), and the products were wrapped in cellophane, rather than paper.[13]

Sweet things represented a rare Soviet food where consumption was roughly comparable across all earning levels.[14] Between 1970 and 1990 production of cakes and confectionery rose by 45 per cent. Cakes, candies and chocolates helped to keep the population sweet in the most literal way.

But buying sweets and cakes in a shop (or trying to) was not the only option for Soviet consumers. Among the tide of advice manuals and booklets aiming to foster 'new traditions' that poured from Soviet presses in the late 1950s was a landmark publication for amateur bakers, *The Home Preparation of Cakes and Pastries, Biscuits, Gingerbreads, and Pies* by Robert Kengis and Pavel Markhel (1959). Previous Soviet publications had allocated at most a few dozen recipes to sweet things. At 368 pages, copiously illustrated, this book was far more ambitious in scope. The colour photographs showed creations that were still more fantastical than those in *The Book of Tasty and Nutritious Food*: layer upon layer of sponge, buttercream, and confectioner's custard, covered with swirls of decoration and icing.

Yet the book was also practical. Where the instructions for *The Book of Tasty and Nutritious Food* were limited, in the case of baking to an unhelpful degree (oven temperatures and cooking times were at best vague), *The Home Preparation of Cakes and Pastries* was meticulous. Both Kengis and Markhel were pastry chefs by trade, and Kengis was an experienced author of manuals for professional bakers. Their recipes gave full lists of ingredients, accompanied by black-and-white photographs precisely illustrating the techniques and equipment required. This was by any standards a superb home baking manual, an incomparably more professional publication than anything previously published for amateur Soviet cooks. If they wanted to serve a 'Kyiv gâteau', an elaborate confection of chocolate-flavoured layered sponge and buttercream, owners of *The Home Preparation of Cakes and Pastries* did not have to rush to a shop, courting disappointment. If they had several hours over two days to spare, they could create a blockbusting delight themselves.

Between 1959 and 1991, the year that the USSR collapsed, *The Home Preparation of Cakes and Pastries* appeared seven times, in editions running to over half a million copies each (the total of all copies printed was over three million). In the USSR, large print runs did not necessarily reflect reader demand. But oral history records that Kengis and Markhel's book was a prized possession in many Soviet households.

At the same time, people continued baking dishes that would have been recognizable to cook-book authors back in the 1840s: deep-fried pastry twists, or 'brushwood', little pastry birds ('larks'), plain sponge loaves like the English madeira cake (keks). But perhaps most characteristic of late Soviet sweet-making was the uncooked assemblage made of crushed biscuits and flavouring, sometimes with cream or condensed milk also, and often with an evocative name: peanut-topped 'anthill', buttercream and biscuit crumb 'hungry dog', dense, solid 'sweet sausage'.[15]

If layer cakes depended on efficient ovens, such 'instant', apparently simple, cakes were indebted to another form of 'technology transfer'. Like their counterparts in Britain, 'fridge cakes', 'anthills' and 'sweet sausage' were a product of domestic refrigerators – and also of working mothers' need to cut down cooking time.

Preparation of sweets also drew extensively on tradition – arguably more so than with other types of dishes. Roast goose stuffed with apples, the pre-revolutionary Easter treat, was a far less familiar dish in Soviet homes than kulich (the brioche-like Easter loaf) or paskha (sweetened curd cheese drained and turned out from a mould). But people were receptive to novelties too. Families who would never have eaten spicy soups such as the Georgian kharcho were perfectly happy to munch on crunchy chak-chak (deep-fried pastry balls soaked in honey), halva, or various types of Middle or Central Eastern sweetmeat.

The history of one of late Soviet Russia's most popular cakes, gâteau Napoléon (tort Napoleon) well illustrates the capacity for adaptation. This was a regular feature of festive occasions, particularly New Year and birthdays.[16] But the striking feature of tort Napoleon, as compared with the ritual stability of Salad Olivier, was that *two* types of cake were so named (see Figure 6.2). Certainly, a Napoleon always had multiple thin layers filled with some kind of sweet cream. But sometimes the filling was whipped cream, sometimes reduced condensed milk, most often, confectioner's custard. More importantly, in some versions the layers were made of crisp pastry (as in a millefeuille) A competing tradition, though, had soft layers of batter cooked briefly in the oven or on top of the stove.

If salads can be relatively simply traced in written sources, the same is not necessarily true of sweet things, which to a significant extent

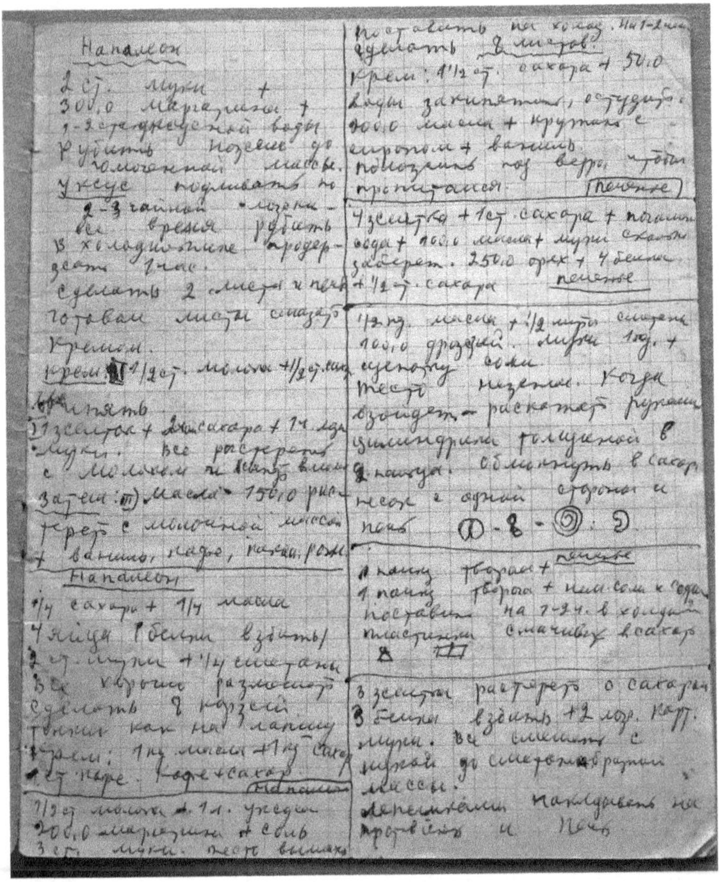

Figure 6.2 Two different recipes for tort Napoleon (top left and bottom left and top right) from a manuscript cookbook (1978). (Courtesy Anna Sokolova.)

existed in parallel to official culinary literature. Children often learned to cook by preparing sweet things (as is true of other culinary cultures also).[17] And family traditions counted for a lot. 'We got all the recipes for pies and biscuits we used by word of mouth. *The Book of Tasty and Nutritious Food* wasn't used for this kind of thing, and if we ever did use it, the results turned out strange and not very nice,' remembered a Muscovite in her forties.[18]

Both Napoleon traditions seem to be rooted in traditions of culinary practice beyond the precision of written texts. The 1901 edition of Molokhovets's book includes a recipe for 'Napoleon Cake', but of a very different kind: a dough made with bitter almonds, rolled thin, cut into fancy shapes and then glazed. Closer to the Soviet tradition is Aleksandrova-Ignatyeva's 'Neapolitan Cake', made of layers of enriched sponge and filled with apricot jam, with knots of baked dough decorated with candied fruit on top. However, the millefeuille type of Napoleon Cake – as served under that name in Ekberg's café in Helsinki, formerly part of the Russian Empire[19] – is not recorded in the most widespread cookbooks. Perhaps it was brought to Petersburg directly by bakers from Finland.

As for the soft version, this is close to what is known in German as Schichtkuchen or Baumkuchen, a cake made of pancake-type layers. A recipe for 'baumkukhen' (the Russian transliteration of the German word) cooked on a spit appeared in Molokhovets's book, and she included it among her suggestions for the Easter feast. However, much closer to the (post-)Soviet Napoleon was another of her recipes, for a 'loaf' (karavai) of pancakes with cream filling. The pancakes were made to Molokhovets's 'ordinary' recipe, then stacked. The filling was made of egg yolks thoroughly beaten with sugar, then mixed with sour cream, and baked in the oven 'till cooked but not separated'.

The key thing about Napoleon in either case was the layers. This echoed expensive shop cakes, but in either version, the cake used modest amounts of butter and cream. If pushed, a cook could make it with ingredients from the store cupboard (one reason for the popularity of condensed milk was its role as an ingredient for quick cake fillings, as well as fridge cakes). Creating Napoleon did not even take an oven. It is probable that the pancake-layer version gained popularity in circumstances where cooking had to be done on a primus, and then became a tradition for some families.

This paradoxical combination of fluidity in the attitude to sweet things and deep attachment to their associations (whether with the personal past or broader social memory) hung on after 1991 as well. Foreign sweet things, particularly Snickers bars, rapidly became so popular as to be naturalized linguistically (snikersy). Yet food nostalgia fixated above all on cakes. Already in 1998, the popular retro programme, *The Old Apartment* (Staraya kvartira) devoted an hour-long episode to the subject of 'torty'. Broadcast mere weeks after the August 1998 default, the programme showed middle-aged Russians luxuriating in happy memories of Soviet-era cakes. With increased panic over E-numbers, the 'state standard' specifications of Soviet days were taken as transcendental indications of quality – even though these in fact permitted the use of additives.

The consumption of sweets was not just about eating. Home-made, these dishes allowed the cook room to demonstrate skill and invention; there was far more variation in the methods of making them and in the ingredients than in the standard dishes of the savoury repertoire (salads, fried or stewed meat, braised vegetables). They were more visually seductive than vegetable or meat dishes, allowing scope for lengthy and complicated decoration. But they also appealed if presented simply (as with berries glowing in their coats of sugar). Finding acceptably tender meat and interesting vegetables took great effort; delicious and unexpected sweets could be conjured from unpromising ingredients (flour, margarine), provided there was a little sugar or honey in hand.

Sweet things could be the instruments of social advancement (as with the gift of a scarce bought cake, available only to those in the inner circle of socialist privilege).[20] But equally well, they could act as aids to solidarity: home-made cakes and biscuits for family parties, a child taught to make a fridge cake as a form of happy socialization. Sweet things bespoke traditional and national values, but people were also welcoming to new ideas.[21] The pining for Soviet sweet things was thus a lament not just for supposedly better-quality buttercream and other signifiers of the 'natural' but for the social contact lost after the USSR collapsed, and in the hectic money-making of the Putin era. Sweets became the symbols of lost communitarianism because community-building had so often been their function in the past.

CHAPTER 7
AFTERWORD: CONSERVING THE PAST, FACED WITH THE FUTURE

In terms of how people define themselves, Russia over the last two and a half centuries has been a conservative food culture. Repudiation of foreign imports (costly, unpalatable, harmful to health) has been widespread. Daily practices, however, have been different. As they moved to cities, former villagers and country landowners adjusted to new foodstuffs, and in due course, to food produced in factories, rather than home kitchens or workshops. Gas stoves edged out solid-fuel stoves. Refrigerators replaced ice houses. Foods that were originally perceived as exotic became familiar and well-loved constituents of the daily diet. These included both raw materials (Far Eastern crabs, kefir, tomatoes, kizil plums and many others) and dishes (plov, khachapuri, chacha, Napoleon gateau, Salad Olivier, frankfurters, and more recently, pizza, hamburgers and sushi).

As novelties were absorbed, they too came to be seen as 'Russian', a process that sometimes resembles less fusion than appropriation. As I was finishing this book, the link between food and empire acquired ugly new associations. After the Russian invasion on 24 February 2022, Ukrainian grain ships in Black Sea ports were blockaded.[1] Crops in occupied territory were confiscated, or subjected to compulsory purchase at knockdown prices, then transported to the Russian Federation, where a hastily created agency, the State Grain Operator, was used to market the expropriated produce, often abroad.

The brazenness of the exercise was in part explained by claims on the part of Vladimir Putin that Ukraine's modern status as a nation state represented a historical absurdity and that the lands where the grain had grown were part of 'New Russia' (Novorossiya), a territory added to the Russian Empire in the eighteenth century. The steppe lands of modern Ukraine should be returned, come what may, to their former role of supplying Russia. If this was tragedy, the battle over borshch in spring 2022 represented farce. After UNESCO added 'the culture of Ukrainian borscht cooking' to its 'List of Intangible Cultural Heritage in Need of Urgent Safeguarding', Maria Zakharova, director of the Russian Foreign Ministry's Information and Press Department, responded by wondering sarcastically when pork would follow. In any case, she claimed, a German traveller of the sixteenth century had observed the eating of borshch among 'the Russians of Kiev'. In 1991, William Pokhlyobkin had expended vast energies on attempting to prove that vodka was a Russian invention; in 2022, questionable history asserted Russian 'ownership' over soup.

There was more than imperial revanchism at stake. The invasion of Ukraine also damaged the food policies operating within Russia since Vladimir Putin took power in 1999. Though food, like construction and city planning, was an area where clientelist relationships flourished (notably, the award of lucrative catering contracts and agricultural subsidies to presidential cronies such as Evgeny Prigozhin), the sector was nevertheless an engine of economic growth – a process helped, rather than hindered, by the counter-sanctions against EU produce in 2014. In the more prosperous areas of Russia, food culture flourished – even formerly rust belt Pskov acquired European-style cafes (see Figure 7.1).

The far wider-ranging sanctions imposed upon Russia in 2022, on the other hand, placed in jeopardy the entire policy of expanded food exports. The situation also accelerated the two-step of rising prices and diminishing choice for consumers, particularly in the middle market, that had been obvious even before the war started (see Figure 7.2). Certainly, there were no real shortages of the kind familiar in the late 1980s and early 1990s, but quality had palpably deteriorated. The handful of newly opened restaurants (often with foreign names, evoking countries and produce now out of reach) had a wan air.[2]

Russia's swerve, from 2014 onwards, into aggressive nationalism hit 'people of the middle state' particularly hard. Among those who

Figure 7.1 Café Misha, Pskov, 2021. Author photograph.

supported the war, outward defiance and resentment towards the supposed causes of the difficulties (Ukraine and the West) covered deeper uncertainties. Those critical of the invasion were increasingly demoralized – so, too, those in favour, as Russia's early battlefield successes began to melt away. For some, it was less food than alcohol which acted as a consolation. If I had finished this book in 2021, the state of Russian food would, in the main, have looked cheering. Now, this area of Russian life, like many others, seems vexed and vulnerable.

Figure 7.2 Food shop interior, St Petersburg, 2022. Author photograph.

NOTES

Introduction

1. T. Kondrat'eva, *Kormit' i pravit': o vlasti v Rossii XVI-XX godov* (Moscow: Rosspen, 2006).

2. This was an international process, of course. As Lizzie Collingham puts it (Lizzie Collingham, *The Hungry Empire: How Britain's Quest for Food Shaped the Modern World* (London: The Bodley Head, 2017), p. 126), 'By the end of the eighteenth century, it seemed perfectly normal to transport potentially perishable food and drink over immense distances.'

3. In fact, rye was expensive in the far north (see Chapter 1), so from nanny's point of view, the pies were special.

4. Paul Freedman, *American Cuisine and How It Got This Way* (New York: W. W. Norton, 2019), p. 150, p. 215.

5. John Dickie, *Delizia! The Epic History of the Italians and Their Food* (London: Simon and Schuster, 2007); cf. Diego Zancani, *How We Fell in Love with Italian Food* (Oxford: Bodleian Library, 2019). See also Anya von Bremzen, *National Dish: Around the World in Search of Food, History, and the Meaning of Home* (New York: Penguin Random House, 2023).

6. The impact of the railways was muted by high costs and inefficiency: 'Our railways charge large sums and transport goods at the speed of ox waggons', complained Pyotr Kuleshov in his 1893 manual on pig management. But the network was vital for transporting livestock, and fresh food for city-dwellers from producers close by.

7. See Chapter 4.

8. See e.g. a secret Leningrad Regional Party Committee report on working-class family budgets from 1963, TsGAIPD-SPb. 25/91/103/37-40, and cf. *RKTB* for the 1890s.

9. Compare the Indian cookbooks discussed in Arjun Appadurai, 'How to Make a National Cuisine: Cookbooks in Contemporary India', *Comparative Studies in Society and History*, vol. 30, no. 1 (1988), pp. 3–24.

Notes

10. RGIA 803/16/2372/11.

11. The materials, archived in the Russian Ethnographical Museum, St Petersburg, have so far been published only in part; nevertheless, *RKTB* is an immensely valuable source for work on food research.

12. *RKTB*, vol. 1, p. 295.

13. 'Garret Life' (1919–1920).

14. See the writings of Olga Merezhkovskaya, e.g. *Advice to Housewives* (*c*. 1950).

15. Political disgrace was a different world: see Yuliya Sokolova, wife of Osip Pyatnitsky, arrested in 1937, who noted in her diary in 1937 queuing for 'kefir and smetana till noon'.

16. The 1972 state standard (GOST) 5-1204-72 for truffle gâteau included vanillin as well as essences and colourings.

17. As Muscovite Antonina Z. recalled in 1972.

18. References to 'wonder pots' on Prozhito.ru go back to the 1940s.

19. This was less true in Belorussia, which local landowners tended to view simply as a backward Russian province.

20. Oleg Amitrov, 3 and 7 June 1985.

21. My thanks to Eleanor Peers at the Scott Polar Research Institute, University of Cambridge, for this information.

22. For instance, GOST 23670–79, 29 May 1979 allowed goat, buffalo and yak in sausages, while GOST 5.1204–72 (1972) for truffle gâteau regulated the results as to moistness rather than proportions of butter, sugar and eggs.

23. Re. the vogue for farm-to-table, it is notable that the most prominent venture, LavkaLavka, which opened in 2009, experienced serious financial difficulties from 2017 and closed four years later.

24. On the other hand, Facebook group 'Ne nravitsya v SSSR' (What I Hate about the USSR) was a vitriolic, and often very funny, antidote.

25. For the point made in the positive (pattern is essential to eating), see Mary Douglas, 'Deciphering a Meal', *Daedalus*, vol. 101, no. 1 (1972), p. 62.

26. Bishop Konstantin Uspensky, 27 July 1854.

27. Agood source on the transformation of classic dishes is Ol'ga and Pavel Syutkin, *Russkaya kukhnya: ot mifa k nauke* (Moscow: Novoe literaturnoe obozrenie, 2022).

Chapter 1

1. See e.g. *RKTB*, vol. 2.2 (Yaroslavl' Province), p. 409: white bread was now the norm in a district where many locals earned money from crafts.

2. The term 'ris', borrowed from French, came into use in the 1830s—1840s; prior to that, and occasionally later, one meets 'sarachenskoe psheno', 'saracen millet'. The change likely reflects a shift to importing via Western Europe rather than directly from Eurasia.

3. *RKTB*, vol. 2, p. 376 (Yaroslavl', with rye). This type of kisel should not be confused with the flour-thickened fruit compote also so named.

4. The root is probably Finnish *leipää* (bread).

5. Tolstoy's story *Polikushka* (1863) shows the heroine making white ones for a holiday.

6. Much of this territory lay in what is now Ukraine and Kazakhstan.

7. At this point, development speeded up: If there were just 200 flour mills across the country in the mid-1880s (A. A. Bakhtiarov, *Bryukho Peterburga: obshchestvenno-fiziologichicheskie ocherki* (St Petersburg: F. Pavlenkov, 1888), p. 200), even a small town well outside the main grain-producing areas such as Novgorod Veliky, with a population of around 28,000, had three flour mills by 1918 (TsGA-SPb. 1200/1/15/12).

8. Bakhtiarov, *Bryukho Peterburga*, pp. 99–140.

9. *Ves' Peterburg* makes it clear that in the 1910s, there were around 700 bakeries of enough size to advertise in a street directory, so likely well over 1000 small ones.

10. TsGA-SPb. 1200/1/36, passim (1919–1920); TsGA-SPb. 1200/1/15/28 (July 1918).

11. GOST 2077–84, https://docs.cntd.ru/document/1200006141.

12. 11 April 1981.

13. I remember having home-made pizza myself in 1985, made with the all-purpose white flour that is still standard in Russia, not bread flour, and baking soda, rather than yeast (hard to buy because of its alcohol-making potential).

14. According to etymologist Max Fasmer, the Russian words for pie (*pirog, pirozhok*) do not actually derive from 'pir' (feast); however, the spelling changed from 'pyrog' to accommodate the vernacular conviction that the words were connected.

15. Eva Felinskaya, for example, wrote on 23 July 1839 about encountering 'chopped beef in a French dough'.

16. This is clear in Volzhin's book, for instance.

17. TsGA-SPb. 9366/1/84/28; ibid., 163/41.

Chapter 2

1. Literally, 'young ram' (*baran mladoi*).

2. Here, Derzhavin copied Horace's equally ambiguous ending.

3. As recorded in *RKTB*: e.g. 'guznostrel' (a local name for 'prostokvasha', a thick yoghourt-like soured milk product). There are many references to 'tvorog', a particularly versatile product as it could be used for pie fillings and bakes.

4. *Byulleten' Sankt-Peterburgskoi skotopromyshlennoi i myasnoi birzhi* for 1914 has daily figures ranging from 1800 to 2500–3500, though during the war arrivals sometimes dropped as low as a few hundred.

5. As *RKTB* indicates, studen' was also eaten in some villages.

6. In the early 1890s, there were eight vendors of 'offal and guts' (gusak i kishki) in the capital (*Ves' Sankt-Peterburg 1893*). The normal meaning of gusak is 'gander'; the derivation is probably sarcastic – offal was at the furthest possible remove from holiday roast goose.

7. See e.g. *RKTB*: vol. 2.1 (Yaroslavl' Province), p. 381.

8. *La bête singulière: les Juifs, les Chrétiens et le cochon* (Paris: Gallimard, 1994). See also Galina Kabakova, 'Aliments interdits, aliments sacrés chez les slaves de l'Est', *Religions et alimentation: Homo Religiosus*, vol. 20 (2019), p. 125, though she also notes exceptions (p. 126).

9. *RKTB*, vol. 3 (Kaluga Province), p. 152, p. 151.

10. The precise date is difficult to gauge because 'syr' was also used for curd cheese (cf. tvorog).

11. *Molochnoe khozyaistvo*, pp. I–IV.

12. Ibid.

13. *RKTB*, vol. 2.1, p. 378; vol. 2.2, p. 136.

14. 'There is a pig in every household', *RKTB*, vol. 3 (Kaluga Province), p. 303; cf. ibid., vol. 1 (Tver Province), p. 417; ibid., vol. 2.1, p. 591; ibid., vol. 2.2, p. 344 (among well-off peasants). Even an informant from Yaroslavl Province who remarked that pork was traditionally taboo added: 'But the peasants are starting to use it more and more for food' (ibid., vol. 2.1, p. 381).

15. *RKTB*, vol. 3 (Kaluga Province), p. 152, p. 151; vol. 2.1 (Yaroslavl Province), p. 591.

16. Important also was Bulgarian scientist Stamen Grigoriev's work with Lactobacillus bulgaricus, which was promoted by Ilya Metchnikoff, born near Kharkiv and director of the Institut Pasteur in Paris.

17. There is a chapter on sour milk products in Brodsky, Kokhan and Shapiro's *The Marketing of Food Products* and they are listed in the annual report from the Leningrad Milk Products Trust, 1940.

18. Aleksei Oreshnikov recalled queuing for forty-five minutes (2 June 1928).

19. 31 December 1932, Oreshnikov.

20. Galkin noted that 50 per cent beef and veal on sale came from animals removed from herds as substandard.

21. See Dimitry Kuznetsov's autobiography of his 1890s childhood recalling how he and his friends' theft of a chicken braising in the oven for a harvest supper attracted severe punishment: RGIA 803/16/2732/19-19 ob.

22. There was experimental work in this area at the All-Soviet Scientific Research and Technological Institute of Poultry Husbandry in Moscow, for example.

23. The Chernyanka facility in Belgorod Province, for instance, had just a refrigerator as a concession to modernity.

24. TsGAIPD-SPb. 24/174/14/6 (1979).

25. Adding bread soaked in milk was acceptable practice 'to lighten' the meat mixture going back to the nineteenth century.

26. See Naiman and Narinskaya.

27. Something else that I remember in Voronezh.

28. TsGA-SPb. 9605/4/71/1-5.

29. Records of such incidents (radiation in Chernivtsi and 500 hen deaths in Donetsk) include secret reports sent by the KGB to the Central Committee of the Ukrainian Communist Party, SBU HA 1/16/1140/140, 166; ibid., 1146/55.

30. TsGAIPD 24/159/5/5, 10, 12.

31. See, for example, the disturbing photograph of the rabbit section at the Tomarovka Meat Plant in rural Belgorod Province, 1984: a worker in blood-stained overalls armed with a cudgel gloatingly holds aloft a terrified rabbit.

32. Moscow Province, 1984. Pers. inf.

Notes

Chapter 3

1. Edwards, for example, provided an *ukha* recipe very like Pushkin's: 'Cut the sterlet in pieces, pour boiling water over it; add salt, spice, and some slices of lemon, and boil.'

2. As recorded by A. Il'in, 17 June 1873.

3. 'Preserve ponds' were uncommon even in Moscow; fish was caught in the river instead.

4. Roman Nazirov, 19 April 1951.

5. Also in 1958, restrictions were introduced on fishing in inland waterways.

6. TsGAIPD-SPb. 25/91/103/38.

7. See Nikolai Kozakov in 1962 (quoted in Introduction).

8. Demyan's Fish Soup is proverbial for over-lavish hospitality, offered till the guest reaches screaming point.

9. A more plausible conjecture is that the model was Estonia's Vanaturg fish shop chain, which held preserved herring tastings seven years before Okean was founded.

10. Three decades after the collapse of the USSR, there were still many internet recipes for Ocean Paste.

11. See the record of questions from the floor to Party agitators, TsGAIPD-SPb. 24/159/2/59.

12. Angling for non-commercial purposes was widely tolerated in the USSR. Even the law of 15 September 1958 that restricted fishing of inland waters explicitly allowed amateurs to fish for free in all public waters that were not nature reserves, fish hatcheries or fish farms, while members of hunting and fishing societies could also use waters leased and maintained by these.

13. Dmitry Pyanov, Artem Delmukhametov, and Evgeny Khrustalev, 'Pike-Perch Farming in Recirculating Aquaculture Systems (RAS) in the Kaliningrad Region', *Foodbalt* 2014, p. 315.

14. *The State of World Fisheries and Aquaculture (SOFIA)*, Food and Agriculture Organization of the United Nations, 2022, Table 2 and Table 5.

Chapter 4

1. The Durnovo household regularly ate ryabchik, and journalist Vladimir Gilyarovsky's *Moscow and the Muscovites* has a vignette of a decayed aristocrat at Khitrovka (Moscow's Skid Row) nibbling a tattered bone: 'But it was ryabchik!'

2. Moroshka (the modern transliteration) is the Arctic raspberry, much prized throughout northern Europe.

3. William Barnes Steveni noted that Russian peasants believed bears were former sinners turned into animals as a punishment, and that reindeers were sacred.

4. Cf. *The Parisian Chef* (1825), Radetsky, S. Rogalskaya, Aleksandrova-Ignat'eva.

5. Lyall saw champignons grown in hotbeds, which likely explains the Russian disdain (to this day, *real* mushrooms are first and foremost wild wood mushrooms).

6. Hunters could also obtain permits directly from the Commissariat of Agriculture, but only if no union existed in their area. In 1926, fees of 1 rouble per year for villagers and 3 roubles for all others were introduced. Between 1926 and 1932, the central hunting management organ shifted to the forestry management bureaucracy, and thereafter to the Foreign Trade Ministry, but in 1933–39 it went back to agriculture.

7. My thanks to Serguei Oushakine for this memory.

8. My thanks to Maria Galina.

9. See Aleksei Vinokurov's note in his diary on 29 May 1942.

10. Arif Saparov, 24 June 1942.

11. A less healthy use for cranberries was encased in sugar, a popular sweet of the late Soviet era.

12. Karelians were more adventurous: cf. mushrooms on a stall at Helsinki market in the late 2010s with an alarming skull and crossbones and instructions to repeat boil. In Russia, this is recorded only in extremis (e.g. Mikhail Smirnov, 23 June 1942, in wartime).

13. See her diary entries, 8 and 9 August 1972 and 10 August 1982.

14. The precise legal phrasing is 'animals entered in the Red Book'.

15. A new law of 22 December 2021 created considerable anxiety about the protection of endangered species, though article 24 of the law on the Animal World was retained in closely similar form.

Chapter 5

1. Gavrila Derzhavin, 'In Praise of Country Life' (1798) (for the quotation, see Chapter 2).

2. In Ukraine, vegetables have traditionally been eaten widely: the early 1920s diary of Anatoly Starodubov, b. 1909, from Dnepropetrovsk (Dnipro) records main dishes such as green aubergine soup, lettuce soup, kasha with marrow, etc.

3. Where the English word 'vegetables' is all-inclusive (though perhaps not extending to 'herbs'), Russian has a number of different terms: 'korneplody' (literally 'root fruits'), 'zelen' ('greens'), 'travki' ('herbs') – the last two categories were traditionally sold in stalls or shops specializing in 'greengrocery' (zelennotorg). 'Ovoshch' is the nearest word to 'vegetable', though in West Slavonic languages, cognate terms (ovoce etc.) mean 'fruit'.

4. Radetsky, for instance, suggested green salad, or a macedoine of stewed vegetables, to accompany cold meats.

5. *RKTB*, vol. 1, p. 340. Cf. ibid., p. 248, p. 295; from Tver Province, ibid., pp. 458–9; vol. 2, p. 377 (Yaroslavl Province).

6. *RKTB*, vol. 2, p. 379 (Yaroslavl Province).

7. *RKTB*, vol. 2, p. 378.

8. *RKTB*, vol. 2, p. 378, citing pancakes made for Shrovetide.

9. *RKTB*, vol. 2, p. 378. Cf. p. 248, p. 591; vol. 3 (Kaluga Province), p. 151.

10. See Introduction.

11. *BTNF* 1952, pp. 43–51, pp. 302–5.

12. According to a Leningrad food inspection report of 1957, 10–15 per cent of canteen salads were contaminated with harmful bacteria: TsGA-SPb 9926/1-1/251/24-5 (by comparison, in the Environmental Standards report of the London Borough of Hammersmith for 2017–18, just 2 out of 136 food samples failed hygiene tests).

13. Likewise, Chekhov's father Pavel noted on 15 May 1896 that he was growing *tomaty* at the writer's Melikhovo estate.

14. Benois, 7 September 1906; on pickles, see Anna Allendorf, 22 October 1906; on 'caviar', Leonid Sayansky, 1 September 1914; on eating raw, Nikolai Druzhinin, 28 June 1913. Prozhito.ru.

15. See e.g. Brodsky, Kokhan, and Shapiro, *The Marketing of Food Products* (1933).

16. The recipes are for breakfast salads, plus adding to mixed vegetables or a garnish for salt herring.

17. *Kulinariya*, pp. 792–4.

18. See e.g. Antonina Z., 15 February 1970, 28 May 1970.

19. See *RKTB*, vol. 2.1, p. 378.

20. Or did, before the Russian invasion of February 2022.

21. Oak is particularly popular because the tannin is supposed to give the pickles the vital extra crunch.

22. In 1939, for instance, tax liability began at 2500 roubles for vegetable gardens and 3500 for orchards, at an overall rate starting at around 10 per cent and rising to 12.5 per cent. Non-members of collective farms paid between 25–45 per cent.

23. In 1963, Leningraders spent just half the amount on fruit that they did on vegetables, a sum already lower than on meat, and much lower than on milk products. TsGAIPD-SPb. 25/91/103/38.

24. In the same way, dried fruit, while available through state shops and public catering, was far inferior to the Uzbek raisins and dried apricots that you could buy in markets.

25. TsGAIPD-SPb. 24/159/2/52.

26. Author's field notes 2010.

Chapter 6

1. Examples included a refinery founded by the Karamzin family on the territory of modern Belgorod Province and by members of the Gendrikov family there and near Kharkiv.

2. *RKTB*, vol. 2.1, p. 382; cf. vol. 3 (Kaluga Province), p. 437. On overall budgets, see vol. 2.2 (Yaroslavl Province), p. 128; on cream puddings, vol. 1 (Kostroma Province), p. 295.

3. Avdeeva's *Pocket Cookbook* (p. 125) includes a recipe made of plain dough and unsweetened curd cheese; Lyubov' Gorovits-Vlasova

(2 June 1903) refers to vatrushki served with jams, sweet things and liqueurs at a pretentious local priest's house.

4. See the diary of historian Mikhail Lemke for February and March 1916.

5. See e.g. Maria Germanova, 1919 (no exact date).

6. See 'Komissar i poet' (1921), by Tsvetaeva's nine-year-old daughter Ariadna Efron, Prozhito.ru. For other references to home baking, see Ol'ga Sivers, 29 November 1918; Aleksei Oreshnikov, 19 April 1922.

7. Boris Sushchenko, 5 September 1933.

8. For instance, Leningrad artist Ivan Petrovsky (16 January 1936) noted three types of layer cake, sponge cakes, fruit paste and braided dough 'krendelya' at tea.

9. TsGA-SPb. 1203/30/80/2 ob., 8, 39. (Samoilova Confectionery Factory, 1939).

10. Tat'yana Grigorova-Rudykovskaya, 25 January 1942; Mariya Mashkova, 14 April 1943; Aleksandr Boldyrev, 24 April 1943. The records of the Samoilova Confectionery Factory indicate that more conventional sweets were also made at this time (TsGA-SPb. 1203/30/169/1-24), but these were likely supplied to the army.

11. Interviews by CK, 2003.

12. See e.g. Mark Kharitonov, 1 October 1977.

13. TsGA-SPb. 203/34-1/12/1-4.

14. See the figures for the 1960s: TsGAIPD-SPb. 25/91/103/38 (range 28.4 roubles p.a. to 31.6 roubles p.a. poorest-richest, though more variation with cakes and confectionery: 35 to 52.1 p.a.).

15. When I organized a mini-survey on Facebook in 2017, ten out of eighty correspondents mentioned these cakes, the third highest score for anything home-made, after gâteau Napoléon (see below) and pies.

16. In my 2017 Facebook survey, twenty-five out of eighty correspondents named it, the highest proportion.

17. My thanks to Olga Smolyak for the point about children.

18. Facebook discussion, 2017.

19. Visit, September 2017.

20. Contributors to my Facebook discussion from Russian provincial cities commented that lavish cakes were simply not available in the shops. I recall that there was a very limited selection of patisserie, mainly cream horns, in Voronezh.

21. This is an important modification to the generally valid case that food has become the instrument of straightforward nationalist politics since the formation of the Russian Federation in 1992.

Chapter 7

1. Limited grain convoys began to be allowed out on a temporary basis in summer 2022.
2. The comments are based on long-term experience as a shopper in St Petersburg, including visits in February and October 2022.

FURTHER READING

(a fuller list will be found on site)

General histories

Alison K. Smith, *Cabbages and Caviar: A History of Food in Russia* (London: Reaktion Books, 2021), places food and cooking in the overall context of Russian history.

Darra Goldstein, *The Kingdom of Rye: A Brief History of Russian Food* (Oakland: University of California Press, 2022), displays a culinary expert's attention to tastes and techniques.

R. E. F. Smith and David Christian's *Bread and Salt: A Social and Economic History of Food and Drink in Russia* (Cambridge, UK: Cambridge University Press, 1984), is authoritative on the areas that it covers.

Susanne A. Wengle, *Black Earth, White Bread: A Technopolitical History of Russian Agriculture and Food* (Madison: University of Wisconsin Press, 2022), traces state control of food production from the late Imperial era to the present day.

Cookbooks

Carla Capalbo, *Tasting Georgia: A Food and Wine Journey* (London: Pallas Athene, 2017).

Lesley Chamberlain, *The Food and Cooking of Russia* (Harmondsworth: Penguin, 1982).

Pamela Davidson, 'Russian Food' in Jane Grigson, *The Observer Guide to European Cookery* (London: Michael Joseph, 1983).

Pamela Davidson, 'Recipes from the Soviet Union' in Alan Davidson, *North Atlantic Seafood* (Harmondsworth: Penguin, 1986).

Darra Goldstein, *Beyond the North Wind: Recipes and Stories from Russia* (Berkeley, CA: Ten Speed Press, 2020).

Olia Hercules, *Mamushka* (London: Mitchell Beazley, 2015).

Olia Hercules, *Kaukasis: A Culinary Journey through Georgia, Azerbaijan, and Beyond* (London: Mitchell Beazley, 2017).

Claudia Roden, *The Book of Jewish Food* (London: Allen Lane, 1997).

Olga and Pavel Syutkin, *CCCP Cook Book: True Stories of Soviet Cuisine*, trans. Ast A. Moore (London: FUEL, 2015).

Alissa Timoshkina, *Salt and Time: Recipes from a Russian Kitchen* (London: Mitchell Beazley, 2019).

Pyotr Vail and Alexander Genis, *Russian Cuisine in Exile*, trans. Angela Brintlinger and Thomas Feerick (Boston: Academic Studies Press, 2018).

Anya von Bremzen, *Mastering the Art of Soviet Cooking* (New York: Crown, 2013).

INDEX

Index

Index